Textual Analysis

In this new book, you'll learn how to teach evidence-based writing using a variety of tools, activities, and sample literary texts. Showing elementary and middle school students how to think critically about what they're reading can be a challenge, but author C. Brian Taylor makes it easy by presenting 12 critical thinking tools along with step-by-step instructions for implementing each one effectively in the classroom. You'll learn how to:

- Design units and lesson plans that gradually introduce your students to more complex levels of textual analysis;
- Encourage students to dig deeper by using the *12 Tools for Critical Thinking*;
- Help students identify context and analyze quotes with the *Evidence Finder* graphic organizer;
- Have students use *The Secret Recipe* strategy to construct persuasive evidence-based responses that analyze a text's content or technique;
- Create *Cue Cards* to teach students how to recognize and define common literary devices.

The book also offers a series of extra examples using mentor texts, so you can clearly see how the strategies in this book can be applied to excerpts from popular, canonical, and semi-historical literature. Additionally, a number of the tools and templates in the book are available as free eResources from our website (www.routledge.com/9781138950658), so you can start using them immediately in your classroom.

C. Brian Taylor serves as a teacher, K-12 ELA coach, and district consultant in the Safford Unified School District and throughout Arizona.

**Other Eye On Education Books
Available from Routledge**
(www.routledge.com/eyeoneducation)

The Common Core Grammar Toolkit:
Using Mentor Texts to Teach the Language Standards in Grades 3–5
Sean Ruday

The Common Core Grammar Toolkit:
Using Mentor Texts to Teach the Language Standards in Grades 6–8
Sean Ruday

The Informational Writing Toolkit:
Using Mentor Texts in Grades 3–5
Sean Ruday

The Argument Writing Toolkit:
Using Mentor Texts in Grades 6–8
Sean Ruday

The Narrative Writing Toolkit:
Using Mentor Texts in Grades 3–8
Sean Ruday

Teaching the Common Core Literature Standards in Grades 2–5:
Strategies, Mentor Texts, and Units of Study
Lisa Morris

Close Reading in Elementary School:
Bringing Readers and Texts Together
Diana Sisson and Betsy Sisson

The Flexible ELA Classroom:
Practical Tools for Differentiated Instruction in Grades 4–8
Amber Chandler

Everyday SEL in Elementary School:
Integrating Social-Emotional Learning and Mindfulness Into Your Classroom
Carla Tantillo Philibert

Learning on Your Feet:
Incorporating Physical Activity into the K-8 Classroom
Brad Johnson and Melody Jones

Textual Analysis Made Easy

Ready-to-Use Tools for Teachers, Grades 5–8

C. Brian Taylor

NEW YORK AND LONDON

First published 2017
by Routledge
711 Third Avenue, New York, NY 10017

and by Routledge
2 Park Square, Milton Park, Abingdon, Oxon, OX14 4RN

Routledge is an imprint of the Taylor & Francis Group, an informa business

© 2017 Taylor & Francis

The right of C. Brian Taylor to be identified as author of this work has been asserted by him in accordance with sections 77 and 78 of the Copyright, Designs and Patents Act 1988.

All rights reserved. No part of this book may be reprinted or reproduced or utilised in any form or by any electronic, mechanical, or other means, now known or hereafter invented, including photocopying and recording, or in any information storage or retrieval system, without permission in writing from the publishers.

Trademark notice: Product or corporate names may be trademarks or registered trademarks, and are used only for identification and explanation without intent to infringe.

Library of Congress Cataloging-in-Publication Data
Names: Taylor, C. Brian, author.
Title: Textual analysis made easy : ready-to-use tools for teachers, grades 5–8 / by C. Brian Taylor.
Description: New York : Routledge, [2017] | Includes bibliographical references and index.
Identifiers: LCCN 2016020522 | ISBN 9781138950641 (hardback) | ISBN 9781138950658 (pbk.) | ISBN 9781315668635 (e-book)
Subjects: LCSH: Critical thinking—Study and teaching (Elementary) | Critical thinking—Study and teaching (Middle school) | Reading (Elementary) | Reading (Middle school)
Classification: LCC LB1590.3 .T28 2017 | DDC 372.47/4—dc23
LC record available at https://lccn.loc.gov/2016020522

ISBN: 978-1-138-95064-1 (hbk)
ISBN: 978-1-138-95065-8 (pbk)
ISBN: 978-1-315-66863-5 (ebk)

Typeset in Palatino
by Apex CoVantage, LLC

For Kena—
A skilled and loving teacher at home and in the classroom

Contents

eResources viii
About the Author ix
Foreword by Jim Blasingame x
Preface xiii
Acknowledgments xv
Introduction xvii

1 **A Critical Thinking Map: Thinking about Text** .1

2 **The 12 Tools** 11

3 **The Evidence Finder** 57

4 **The Secret Recipe** 66

5 **Guided Practice** 73

6 **Extra Examples Using Mentor Texts** 105

7 **Bonus Tool: Cue Cards to Teach Literary Terms** 135

   References 151
   Index 153

eResources

As you read this book, you'll notice the eResources icon (👁) next to the following tools. The icon indicates that these tools are available on our website as free downloads, so you can easily print them for classroom use. The eResources include the following:

Figure 1.4: A Critical Thinking Map (Children's Version) .... page 6
Figure 2.11: Evaluation: Validity & Reliability of a Text .... page 33
Figure 2.16: Analyzing Text: Make a List .... page 37
Figure 2.17: Analyzing Text: Find a Link .... page 38
Figure 2.20: Analyzing Context .... page 40
Figure 2.21: The Profiler .... page 41
Figure 2.30: The 12 Tools (Student Version) .... page 48
Figure 2.32: Thinking FRAME (Blank Template) .... page 50
Figure 3.4: Evidence Finder 1.0 .... page 62
Figure 3.5: Evidence Finder 2.0 .... page 63
Figure 3.6: Evidence Finder 2.1 (Text to Self) .... page 63
Figure 3.7: Evidence Finder 3.0 .... page 64
Figure 3.8: Evidence Finder 4.0 .... page 64

You can access the eResources by visiting the book product page on our website: www.routledge.com/9781138950658. Click on the tab that says "eResources" and select the files. They will begin downloading to your computer.

About the Author

C. Brian Taylor has a PhD in Curriculum and Instruction English Education from Arizona State University (ASU), where he credits Dr. Jim Blasingame and Dr. Alleen Nilsen, along with Dr. Jean Boreen of Northern Arizona University (NAU), for giving him opportunities to learn and serve in the English education community.

Dr. Taylor currently serves as both a classroom teacher and a K-12 ELA coach in the Safford Unified School District in southeastern Arizona, daily mentoring and modeling reading and writing instruction at various grade levels across the curriculum. It's common for Dr. Taylor to sing mnemonic songs that teach sentence fluency with second graders, to extract multi-source evidence to compose critical responses with sixth graders, to analyze fate and free will in Shakespeare's *Macbeth* and to synthesize peer-reviewed journals on cyclones in a science class with high school students—all in the same day. His methods are held in high regard as in-the-trenches practical and highly effective, while his down-to-earth humor and natural rapport leave districts laughing while learning. He enjoys presenting at state and national conferences as often as occasion permits, especially with his wife Kena (also an English teacher) when they are not too busy raising their five children together.

Foreword

I first met Dr. Brian Taylor when I was a new assistant professor at Arizona State University and he was a classroom teacher at Westview High School in the West Valley of greater metropolitan Phoenix. I was so impressed with the innovative and effective approaches Dr. Taylor was using at Westview, especially in his remediation class for students who had failed Arizona's standardized test, the Arizona Instrument to Measure Standards (AIMS), that I asked him to give a presentation on the curriculum he had designed at our annual Arizona English Teachers' Association (AETA) convention. Although the writing portion of the AIMS test had proven to be a stumbling block to graduation for these students, Dr. Taylor did what great teachers throughout the ages have done: he demystified what learners perceived as an impenetrable mystery by breaking it down into its important components and providing effective tools for successfully conquering each part. In *Textual Analysis Made Easy*, Dr. Taylor once again demystifies some of the most common mysteries plaguing our classrooms, providing the tools for teachers to bring their students to high levels of proficiency in writing fluency, correct use of conventions, evidence-based textual analysis, and critical thinking.

Dr. Taylor went on to become a pillar in the English language arts education community, not only in Arizona, but in the US, presenting program after program, not only at AETA but also at the National Council of Teachers of English Annual Conference. Record-breaking numbers of participants poured into Dr. Taylor's workshops at these conventions, as word spread about a classroom teacher whose systematic approach to conducting writing conferences, teaching literary analysis, teaching grammar and usage, and workshopping all genres of writing, provided an adaptable method for meeting state standards and preparing students for standardized test, but more than that for success in college and career.

At this point, I realized our Arizona State University English Education doctoral program would benefit tremendously from having Brian Taylor among our students. We invited Brian in, and just as predicted, he was among the most innovative and productive PhD students in the history of the program. In the ASU doctoral program, Dr. Taylor proved to be passionate about helping teachers move from theory to practice. He heavily researched how pedagogical practices, informed by theoretical concepts, work in the real classroom, not matter how much failure students may have experienced previously. He did his doctoral research and wrote his dissertation on the best concrete practices for conducting teacher/student writing conferences that prepare students for college-level writing. The recommendations in Dr. Taylor's dissertation's final chapter continue to show up in the curriculum and instruction models he designs, and the research methods he employed in earning his PhD continue to serve him well he examines, tests, and refines instructional strategies to meet today's educational challenges.

Textual Analysis Made Easy targets what Wiggins and McTighe call "deep understanding" in their landmark work, *Understanding by Design* (Pearson, 2006). Deep understanding means learning that rises to the mastery of key concepts, big ideas, and the highest level of transfer of the learning to new and unfamiliar contexts. As national shifts in curriculum and instruction call for greater rigor, global employability, and attention to 21st century skills, critical thinking overlays all aspects and is at the center of college and career readiness as defined by state after state across the country; however, how to teach students to think critically remains a very abstract concept with little methodology available to the classroom teacher involving specific instructional strategies, classroom activities, informal and formal assessment instruments, benchmarks, and appropriate adjustments to instruction. Dr. Taylor has developed and refined a step-by-step means for teaching critical thinking by modeling the thinking process much as Nancie Atwell talks about the teacher "taking off the top of his/her head" during the composing process so that students can hear and understand the thought process in which a proficient writer engages. Similarly, Dr. Taylor provides the means through flowcharts, a 12 point tool kit, and step-by-step examples applied both generically and to specific literature selections for teachers to model the critical thinking process to students, enabling those students to do careful, thoughtful, critical analysis of texts. The graphics in this book are invaluable, not only enabling visual learners to conceptualize critical thinking and textual analysis, but also providing a map by which learners can go back to a prior step if they feel uncertain or lost.

A good teacher breaks an authentic task down into its component parts, facilitates the learner in mastering them and then helps them to put it all back together again into a meaningful whole. Dr. Taylor's Question Starters show teachers how to ask thought provoking questions that students will internalize as they climb Bloom's Taxonomy while analyzing a text. Again, the choices are myriad and teachers can model entering and exiting the question and answer method of analysis as they work their way through the thought process in engaging with a text.

Textual Analysis Made Easy comprises Dr. Taylor's journey as a teacher, sharing the results of his research, not only as a scholar but more importantly as a classroom teacher. Other books have pieces of the puzzle for teaching the English language arts, meeting the standards, and shifting instruction to focus on evidence-based writing and evidence-based textual analysis, and critical thinking, but none put it all together in a logical, well-explained plan for designing curriculum and implementing instruction. I congratulate the author on creating an invaluable resource for teachers and thank him for the analytic approach he takes to teaching.

—Jim Blasingame

Preface

Growing up in the southwestern United States, I have listened to pioneer stories most of my life, and it seems fitting to compare my experience as a teacher to a slow and steady wagon train rolling across the plains. Sometimes uneventful, other times adventurous, my true journey as a teacher began when I offered to sit and visit with a student one-on-one. I could not have predicted that this singular conference about a student's writing would, like the single turn of a wagon wheel, change the landscape of my entire career.

Over many years now I have had the privilege of sitting with students one-on-one—as nearly as I can estimate, between eight and nine thousand times—to discuss line by line their paragraphs or essays, what districts often call performance assessments or benchmarks. Normally in such conferences, a student and I would meet individually during class (or by appointment) two or three times per semester in planned 10–20 minute intervals, though length could vary per assignment or student. Our goal was to exchange ideas, ask questions, celebrate successes, and explore potential changes that might enhance the paper substantively and aesthetically toward a final copy.

In my conversations with students, gradually I began to see patterns emerge: common gaps in both their content knowledge and my teaching. At first I probably focused on their sentence fluency and grammar more than their ideas and content. Perhaps I reasoned: How can I invite my students to think critically when their basic sentences are so subpar? More accurately, I probably wasn't even aware of how to get them to think beyond the obvious. Deeper-level thinking can seem so far away when poor writing (or teaching) skills hide such potential. One-on-one writing conferences with students, however, began to reshape my understanding of writing and my role as a teacher.

Like Straub, I wanted to be more than a "reader, facilitator, or coach." I, too, wanted to "make comments that [were] tough, incisive and critical . . . not only friendly and helpful . . . [but] expectant and proving . . . with conversations that [were] at once relaxed and serious" (381). The method of conferencing I embraced felt natural, focused, and open—like it was more than a textbook technique but something that spoke to the core of what education should be. And the immediate results were evident: my rapport with students increased; the substance, depth, and accuracy of their compositions increased; and students' appreciation for themselves and their writing increased. Clearly I had come to find a method that worked for me and seemingly for them.

From these conversations came tools in three prominent areas: (1) sentence fluency and conventions, (2) evidence-based writing, and (3) critical thinking. The latter two are the focus of this book. As teachers we often want to require evidence-based writing and analysis (and know that we should), but we find the topic difficult to express and are unsure how to frame our lessons to increase critical thinking and writing. Standards are replete with such requirements, yet literature on the topic feels somewhat removed from the classroom.

When I look for a resource, I cannot escape practical needs every teacher must consider: Is the method easy to use? Is it flexible if I want to make changes? Is it effective? Can I use it tomorrow? Questions like these serve as important filters for this book. Hopefully tools I introduce will be user-friendly for you.

Acknowledgments

I would like to thank my wife, Kena (Winder) Taylor, for her unwavering support as a friend and colleague, field-testing a number of methods for efficiency and clarification. I would also like to thank my children: my daughter, Jessica, 18, who took pictures used to demonstrate critical thinking in Chapter 2; and in the same chapter, my son, Andrew, 15, and his friends Aaron Judd and Frank Gutierrez for having staged the basketball picture (featured left, center, and right, respectively); my other daughter, Madison, 13, who appears in a picture as herself supposedly sleeping in class (when she is actually a very astute student); and, my sons, Lincoln, 9, and Luke, 7, in the staged bullying picture (they're actually best friends). I can always count on my family to be good sports.

To my Routledge editor, Lauren Davis: I appreciate your warm rapport and critical insight. This book is better because of you. And Marlena Sullivan, thank you for your editing efforts on behalf of this volume. I would like to thank Mike Crockett of Eastern Arizona College, who provided valuable insight on the Thinking about Text: A Critical Thinking Map, as it helped me shape and clarify elements that I would have missed otherwise. The very talented illustrator Wes Hargis took my rough sketch and created a delightful children's version of the critical thinking map in Chapter 1. His young but very skillful daughter Arrow Hargis also drew a number of fun cue card sketches, including the car, tornado, rose, camera, earth, and others. I'm glad that you were able to work with your dad—and mom, Debbie—all of you exceptional artists. Thank you. I would also like to thank Tony Gatewood for providing the Goldilocks and the Three Bears assignment-idea mentioned in Chapter 5; San Carlos Secondary is lucky to have you as a brilliant and inspiring teacher. To Mark Bily formerly of the Flagstaff Unified School District; Superintendent Sherry Dorathy, English teachers Carol Rios, Bill Johnson, and Golda Clark of Miami School District, I remember; and matriarch Lynn Edens and all my collegial family at Westview High School, if this book finds you, thank you so very much. I also recognize teacher Wanda Evans of Safford Unified School District, who suggested adding the line "I want to find evidence of" atop the Evidence Finder, focusing children's attention even more; and of the same district superintendents Dr. Mark Tregaskes and Mr. Ken VanWinkle, Principal Rich DeRidder, and Curriculum Director Henry Dunkerson for providing me a cross-curricular position where I have learned so much. I would also like to extend special thanks to the life-long educator Lance Huffman, who has believed in this material (and in me) from the very beginning. It has been my privilege to have you as a friend. To my student Angelina Garcia, thank you for taking time to draw the footprints for the "foot" cue card in Chapter 7. Artist Brandt Woods provided an effective drawing in Chapter 2. And finally, I would like to thank Pima High School students Kiah Morris and Hallie Shupe for allowing me to use a picture of their cheerleading at a football game.

Introduction

Instead of featuring heavy prose or extensive source citation, this book's focus is one of practical application: it introduces tools and examples with a ready-to-use design meant to simplify critical thinking practice in the classroom. The desired result is to have students be able to write an evidence-based response that analyzes a text's content or technique.

Methods discussed in the opening chapters of this book are simple to use and may be taught in any order, regardless of chapters as they are currently outlined, with one notable exception being the recommended teaching of the Evidence Finder and Secret Recipe in that order. Some teachers begin with the Evidence Finder and Secret Recipe because they have a student-friendly structure to write a response; then, as a means to deepen those responses, they move on to The 12 Tools. Other teachers prefer using the map as a foundation to create questions or writing prompts. Still others prefer starting with the Literary Cue Cards prior to having their class complete an Evidence Finder, so students know what to look for in a text. Whatever the order, these tools seem to work well as an integrated whole. Begin slowly and allow mastery to dictate pacing. Even a hammer—a simple tool—can be painful when an anxious swing is misplaced.

Chapter 1   A Critical Thinking Map: Thinking about Text

Start here if you would like to explore a little of what it means to design a question carefully. I grew up around construction sites. To me, the difference between a carpenter and a craftsman is likely to be found in the level of attention to detail. So it is with teachers. Master teachers understand the art of how to ask questions that naturally lift their students' conceptual understanding from one scaffold to another.

In this chapter you will be introduced to a critical thinking flow chart or map. At first glance, it may appear complicated like any diagram might for someone unfamiliar with the terrain. However, with a little practice, the map should—at least—acclimate teachers to important questions when designing a response to text. Certain combinations (of Steps 1–3 on the map) create the equivalent of highways, or familiar approaches to examine a text; however, if you choose less familiar combinations, the equivalent is more like textual off-roading, which can be equally beneficial and interesting for students. Be patient. The more critical-thinking combinations (or pathways) on which you venture to take your students, the better it will be for them. While the flow chart or map may be projected for students to see, it is primarily a reference for teachers. The illustration "Driving the Text" (where the car represents the text) is less intimidating. If the map is an orientation tool, then the list of Question Starters at each of Bloom's taxonomic levels should provide a kind of compass to practice those certain skills. Questions are sometimes hybrids, mixing more than one cognitive level, but the list should provide an easy reference when designing units, lesson plans, assessments, or—for our purpose here—textual prompts.

Chapter 2   The 12 Tools

Originally a byproduct of conferencing and now a curricular staple, the "12 Tools" provide an easy reference for regular critical thinking practice. What makes these tools unique is the way they are compiled and applied. This book will demonstrate how to use them first with pictures and then with written text. When starting with pictures, students seem to enjoy a nonthreatening way to participate in class. Sentence Starters in both instances (whether showing a picture or written excerpt) help students gain confidence as they practice. Teachers may choose one or more approaches, each of which is introduced in this chapter: one tool at a time, using respective one-page mini-tutorials; all the tools at once, using (examples from) a sample slide presentation that you can create; or at a glance, using one-page tool sheets provided inside. Tools in full view for student reference will encourage regular critical thinking.

Chapter 3   The Evidence Finder

Once the Critical Thinking Map and/or 12 Tools have helped you design a question or activity, students will then gather evidence to support a claim. The Evidence Finder, perhaps the most deceptively helpful tool in this book, is really an evidence organizer, but it positions information for effective use in a paragraph to follow (using The Secret Recipe). This book provides a few blank templates that may be replicated (or adapted in digital form) for your classroom only. You may choose to adapt them based on the nomenclature familiar to your school or district. In this chapter, completed Evidence Finders illustrate the process.

Chapter 4   The Secret Recipe

This portion of the book will then demonstrate how to take evidence organized in an Evidence Finder and use it to create a solid single- or multi-quote/multi-source response. Paragraphs have subtle functions inside them, and this piece offers students one highly effective way to learn those functions. This simple writing structure makes for an effective supporting paragraph or short answer response—a baseline paragraph which can then be deepened using The 12 Tools.

Chapter 5   Guided Practice (for Teachers)

Baseline examples serve as guided practice using tools introduced in Chapters 1–4. Samples follow a step-by-step format so as to encourage parallel processes in your own classroom.

Chapters 6   Extra Examples Using Mentor Texts

A range of sample Evidence Finders and accompanying paragraphs focus on ideas, others on technique. The goal is to provide a cross-section of possibilities using familiar texts that will encourage similar practice. Use them as a model or adapt them to your own text as may benefit your class best. Mentor texts include popular, canonical, and seminal-historical literature.

Chapters 7   Bonus Tool: Cue Cards to Teach Literary Terms

Cue Cards are like giant flash cards placed around the room. Each card utilizes a mnemonic to make terms simpler and more memorable. A miniature version of those cards is included in this book and makes a great practice packet for students. Teachers simply select which ones they want to include and skip the others.

1

A Critical Thinking Map: Thinking about Text

Text in a specific sense is something written, but keep in mind that text can really comprise any artifact through which we communicate or engage our world. With that said, most teachers simply want to know how to get their students to think deeply about written words. You may want to look at the Critical Thinking Map (Figure 1.1) at this point, while I describe it here. See also the Children's Version (Figure 1.4). To begin with a brief overview, you have three decisions to make as a teacher:

Step 1: Choose to Examine the *Text* or *Context* (or both)

TEXT: If you choose to examine the text, you will have your students critically weigh *what* the author said (think ideas and content) or *how* the author said it (think *medium or technique*: organization, sentence fluency, word choice, voice, and conventions; or most literary devices). Figurative language seems to comprise a hybrid exploration examining the relationship between content *and* technique. Regarding what are called the six traits, many fine resources have been published by the Northwest Regional Educational Laboratory (NWREL), now Education Northwest, and developed to discuss these areas, precluding a need here to do anything but recommend their use. Other areas of the country or parts of the world use different nomenclature as indicated by popular, synonymous subscripts in parentheses in the expanded version (see Figure 7.10, p. 149). While designed as an orientation tool for teachers or administrators who want to design questions, benchmarks, assignments, or assessments more carefully, teachers may project a digital version on the board to explain the combination(s) or pathway(s) your students will be taking as you examine a text.

CONTEXT: If you choose to examine the **context**, you will have your students critically think about **who** said it, **to whom**, **when** it was said, **where** it was said, and **why** it was said (or the author's motivation). An important distinction will surface in a later chapter as we teach students how to introduce a quotation from the text. What I am calling *narrative* context (after narrator) is the **context of the author**; what I am calling *literary or dialogic* context (after dialogue) is the **context of the character**.

Step 2: Choose a Learning Process

Learning may be understood as *knowing* something and *doing* something with that knowledge. For my purposes here, I mean to define *knowing* as the learning one obtains through **study** and *doing* as an act of **faith**, the learning one obtains through the literary equivalent of the scientific method or evidence-based inquiry. As we often do not know if our theory or creation or test (in this case, our literary analysis or other reader response) will prove true or actually work, we move forward anyway. It is that act of responding to a text without knowing if we are entirely right that enables learning. Faith as reader response, then, means to step into the unknown, the potentially flawed or problematic, and with limitations still make the attempt.

When selecting a cognitive or learning process, it usually means first establishing a foundational awareness of something—*knowing* it: in simple terms, to define it, to explain it, to take it apart. The most common order of approach is from left to right, but different assignments naturally vary. For example, by *disassembling* something first, it can help a person *understand* something afterward. A teacher might have a student analyze a song and then listen to it, providing both an alternative sensation as well and increased comprehension. Generally teachers have an awareness of Bloom's taxonomy and its iterations. If not, a starting point is to ask questions or design activities that first foster students' basic knowledge and comprehension of the text; the map (and the accompanying "Question Starters") illustrate their basic differences. Next, to analyze something is to take it apart, to identify its pieces and relationships.

A Critical Thinking Map

Figure 1.1 Thinking about Text: A Critical Thinking Map

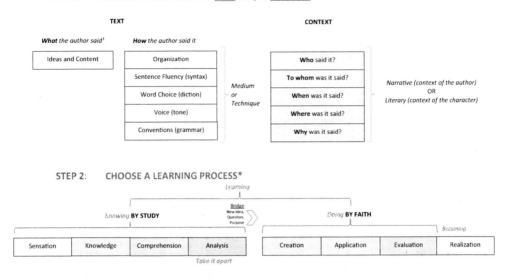

Figure 1.2 Knowing (by Study)

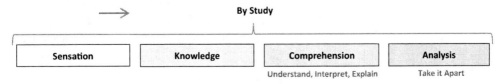

Figure 1.3 Doing (by Faith)

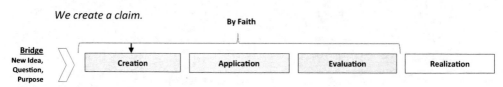

Crossing the Bridge from *Knowing* to *Doing*

If a student can define something, explain it, and articulate its parts, structure, and relationships, then the student is ready to do something with that information. They are ready to create, apply, or evaluate. These learning processes are also non-linear. A learner may select any of the three and move around as needed. Usually a question or purpose (like to solve an authentic problem) invites our learners to cross the **bridge** from the **study** side of *knowing* to the **faith** side of *doing*. We *create* a claim.

Indeed, when we ask "creation" questions (like *Why?*), we invite our students to propose a hypothesis, for which they then gather evidence from a single source or integrate evidence from multiple sources (including their own lives), allowing their theses to change accordingly. They produce a response or solution to answer the teacher's question or solve an observable problem or gap. Exemplary teachers help students understand how they can *apply* their knowledge or creation in their own lives (at home, work, school, or play) and *evaluate* what they create, so as to make improvements or clarify understanding.

To explain "learning processes" to younger students, perhaps the following example as it relates to car mechanics will simplify it for them:

Knowledge: A student at this stage knows the parts of the engine. He or she can look at pictures and match car parts with their names or uses.

Comprehension: A student at this stage can explain how the engine functions. For example, the student can explain how the fuel, mechanical, or electrical systems work independently or together.

Analysis: A student is here when he or she can take apart an engine, list or classify those parts in various groupings. If a car has problems, this student can trouble-shoot by listing *possible* causes of the problem and what affects it might have on performance. (The moment he or she develops a theory of the problem, that student has crossed the bridge into creation because he/she has formed a hypothesis.)

Now the student has a choice to make (crossing the bridge):

Creation: The student may want to build an engine (by fixing or replicating an *old* one); rebuild one, possibly with parts or designs from other cars ("integration" or "inter-synthesis"); or invent an entirely *new* engine. (Innovation may represent the highest form of creation.)

Application: The student may apply his *prior* knowledge by getting a job as a mechanic, or by working on his or her own car.

Evaluation: The student can evaluate the *old engine* (from which he/she learned) or *new* engine (he/she built), testing either to see if it works correctly (validity) and consistently (reliability). Maybe there's a way to make the car more fuel efficient or cost effective. If the student-mechanic then offers a recommendation based on this evaluation, then he or she organically returns to "creation" because a claim has been made.

Sensation and *Realization* indicated on the map are mentioned only briefly in this book, though a teacher may explain how listening to an engine (a sensation) can prove a helpful diagnostic, or the joy of becoming a mechanic (realization) a meaningful endeavor. Once a teacher has selected a text or context (Step 1) and a learning process (Step 2), he or she is ready for students to engage a specific skill.

Step 3: Ask a Question (or Select a Skill)

To design a question carefully is to explore a text deeply; in other words, one targeted question may be more valuable than a bundle of superficial ones. Each time we select a different combination of Steps 1–3, we invite a unique critical thinking pathway. And when students use multiple tools to shape their responses—a technique I refer to in my classes as *"stacking"* their analysis—their depth of knowledge increases, and hopefully their responses do as well. This *stacking* will be demonstrated for you later in the literary analyses chapters (and *Thinking* FRAMES in Chapter 2).

Corresponding Question Starters for each learning process are provided on the following pages for your convenience. Selecting a variety of questions along the path will help students engage a text in sundry ways. Not every question needs to be asked to have a successful curricular unit, but designing a productive one will inevitably employ a healthy cross-section of these

Figure 1.4 A Critical Thinking Map (Children's Version)

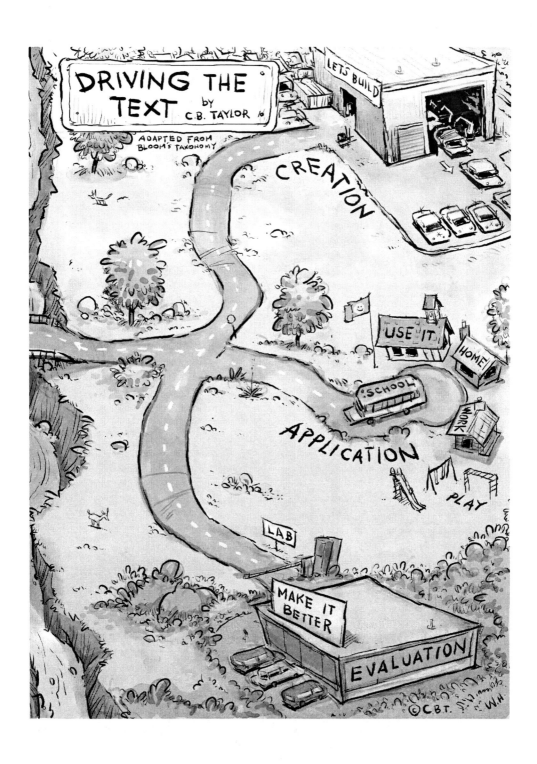

Figure 1.5 Question Starters

(i)

KNOWLEDGE

Recall: Prior Knowledge
What do we already know (or **not** know) about ____?
What did the author say?
Fill in the blank.
(Questions with concrete answers)

Mimic, Copy:
Copy (word for word)/mimic the following ____.

Define:
What is (or write) the definition(s) of ____?
What is the denotation of ____?
Provide a synonym/antonym for ____.
What is the root, word family, or etymology of the word/concept?
Match ____ with its definition.

Describe:
Describe ____. OR How would you describe ____?
Draw a picture of ____.
THE SENSES: *Some form of these questions:*
   What do you see?
   What do you observe?   (Tool 1 See, Don't See)
   What do you hear?
   What do you taste?
   How does it feel to the touch?
   How does it smell?
   What do you **not** [see, hear, taste, feel, or smell]?

Memorize and Recite:
Memorize ____.
Recite ____.

Change:
How does ____ change?
   Explicit = knowledge
   Implicit = comprehension
How does ____ *not* change?   (Tool 2 Change)
   Dynamic = changes
   Static = remains the same
   Extra Note:
      Ending situation
      − Beginning situation
      = Change (which is likely the theme)

COMPREHENSION

Discern Fact from Opinion:
Is ____ true or untrue?   (Tool 3 Agree or Disagree?)
   How do you know? (EVIDENCE)
Is ____ a fact or opinion?
   How do you know? (EVIDENCE)
Is it valid?
Can we trust the source? (to Evaluation)

Interpret:
When the author says/uses ____, what might it **symbolize**?
When the author **figuratively** says/uses ____, what might he/she be really saying?
What is the **connotation** of ____?
When the author says/uses ____, what might he/she be **implying**?
When the author says/uses ____, what can we **infer**?
Translate the following...
Make a visual-audio-digital representation to interpret ____.
Create an analogy to represent ____.   (Tool 4 Says This, Means That)
Explain the real meaning of ____.

Explain or Paraphrase:
Explain ____.
   Explain the concept, event, evidence.
Paraphrase ____.
   Paraphrase the excerpt or evidence.
Put ____ into your own words.
Make a visual representation (chart, graph) of ____.

Summarize: Intra-synthesis[1]:
Summarize ____.
Annotate ____.

Solve in Isolation[2]:
Complete the following textbook problems...
What is the answer to problem #____?
Practice the following ____.

---

[1] To summarize is to demonstrate comprehension, but it also means to "create" a new text from within, hence the "intra-synthesis" label.
[2] To practice in isolation seems to demonstrate comprehension but may also be understood as isolated application (in preparation for holistic or field application).

A Critical Thinking Map ◆ 9

(ii)

Bridge →

ANALYSIS — Take it apart

Lists and Links

List: Identify and Label
CLOSE READING
  Identify/Label ____.
  Highlight ____.
  Underline ____.
  Mark ____.
  Star or place an asterisk next to ____.
  Put a box/circle around ____.

Tool 5 — Make a List

List: See Tool #5, page 17, Lists and Links
Let's make a list of the author's/text's ____.
  Examples:
  Ideas & Content (e.g. Themes or motifs, Ideas, Events, Decisions, Alternatives, Purposes, Characters
  Organization (e.g. Steps, Structures, Outline)
    How is ____ organized?
      - Beginning, Middle, End
      - Plot
      - Topical
      - Chronological
      - Sequential
      - Cause & Effect
      - Problem & Solution
      - Compare & Contrast

Tool 6 — Find a Link

Link: Compare-Contrast
Compare and/or Contrast ____ and ____.

Type of Similarity / Difference = Relationship

What type of relationship/ connection do you see?
  - symbolic   - social (family, friends, etc.)
  - racial   - graphic, structural, geographic
  - professional   - linguistic, behavioral
  - economic   - physical, temporal
  - academic   - ethical, moral, legal
  - spatial   - religious, spiritual

Link: Causation (Cause and Effect)
What caused ____? Why?
Are there potential causes we don't see?
What are the possible effects of ____? Why?
Are there effects we don't see?
Are there continuing effects?
Are there overlapping causes/ effects?
  Note: To speculate or predict is to create.

Link: Correlation
Is there a correlation between ____ and ____?
Is there a pattern between ____ and ____?
Why is this pattern **not** causation?

CREATION — Create a Claim

Propose an Idea
With a Question, Prediction or Claim

If __A__, then __B__.

  B¹ = what will likely happen?
  B² = what could that mean?
  B³ = what may have happened previously?

  B¹ = FUTURE
  B² = PRESENT
  B³ = PAST

If __B__, then __C__.

Tool 7 — If, Then

Note: To create a claim, often a student restates the teacher's question in declarative form, adding a reason or rational (persuasion) or evidence (argument). The conditional "If" is helpful but not required.

Speculate
What can ____ do?
What could ____ have done differently?
What could/might have happened? (deduction)
What would ____ have done/ happened differently (under different circumstances)?

Tool 8 — Should- Would- Could

Empathize
How might ____ (think/feel) in this situation?
When we consider ____ point of view, what do we learn?
How might ____ regard this situation?

Tool 9 — Another's Point of View

Integrate (Inter-synthesis)
What are our resources?
Let's gather and document sources on the topic.
How can we use these other sources/materials to create a new invention/claim?

Produce and Adapt
What can we create (or build) from this?—a new example, tool, technique, or method?
How can we replicate/manufacture ____?
How can we take what we already have and reshape or reconfigure it? Revise or edit it?

Recommend (from Evaluation)
What should ____ do?
What should ____ have done instead?
How should we improve ____?

10 ◆ A Critical Thinking Map

(iii)

APPLICATION

Use, Reuse, Recycle
How can we use ____?
How can we reuse ____?
How can we repurpose ____?
How can we transfer use of ____ to ____?
How can we apply ____ to our own situation?
How can we recycle ____?
How can we **avoid** using ____?

Tool 10 Application

Internalize or Personalize
How can we (use/apply) ____ to our own lives?
How can we transfer use of/apply ____ to ____?
How can you use ____ at home, school, play, or work?—in the "real world"?
How does it **not** apply?

Tips:

Good teachers know that one hallmark of successful education is when students ask—or even better, *design*—the question. You could have pairs or small groups of students use these "question starters" to form their own textual questions.

When you ask a *why* question, you are inviting a student to cross the bridge into "doing" something, in this case forming a hypothesis—and that means rationale or evidence (see Chapter 3 "The Evidence Finder").

To spend time on one thoughtful question may mean "covering" less but "uncovering" more. It implies potentially shrinking the number of questions in a unit so that you may have time to explore greater depth within a single question.

EVALUATION
Make a scale or rubric

Rank: Grade, Assess, Prioritize
What **grade** would you give ____?
On a **scale** of ____, where would you place ____?
Rank/place these in **order** of ____.
Let's make a scoring rubric for ____.

Tool 12 Ranking

Validity[3]
Are our results accurate?
How can we test them to make sure?
Does the claim match the evidence?
Is author bias present?—If so, is it clearly stated?
What do others with experience or expertise say?

Reliability
Are our results consistent?
How can we (or someone else) repeat the test to see if the same result is achieved?

Importance or Quality
Rank these ____ according to priority (or importance).
Place these ____ in order of good, better, best.
Place these ____ in order of bad, worse, worst.
How much better/worse would ____ make ____?
Rank these ____ according to (a certain) quality.

Efficiency
Rank these ____ in order of efficiency.
Place these ____ in order of fastest to slowest.
How might ____ be more efficient?

Effectiveness
Is/was ____ (effective/ineffective) at ____?
How might ____ be more effective at ____?
Rank these ____ in order of effectiveness.

Tool 11 Effective-Ineffective

Difficulty, Effort
How hard will it be to ____?
What's an easier way of doing it?
Rank these ____ in order of difficulty/effort.

Strength
Rank these ____ in order of strength/weakness.
Create a scale/rubric that weighs the strength or weakness of ____.

Cost, Benefits
What is the least expensive way to ____?
Rank these ____ in order of potential cost/reward.

[3] *Discerning* validity and *testing the degree* of validity illustrates the close connection between comprehension and evaluation, respectively.

(or similar) questions. Obviously this list of questions and prompts is not meant to be exclusive, only a good starting point (and some may overlap). Text-dependent questions make for good reader-responses. The 12 Tools (circled) are added for reference later and provide an abridged but easily accessible list of questions as well. Following this introduction to "A Critical Thinking Map: Thinking about Text" is an introduction to critical thinking tools, dubbed The 12 Tools, which give learning processes kid-friendly (and hopefully memorable) names.

2
The 12 Tools

Whenever I teach students about "deeper-level thinking," I use an analogy of learning to swim. Maybe it's because many of these elementary and middle school students enjoy the activity, and it suits my point: when we first learn to swim, we stay in the shallow end because we want to feel safe. But the moment we can swim from side to side, we are immediately drawn to the deep end of the pool. We want to go off the diving board. We want to touch the bottom. We want to explore. The same is true for *thinking*: at first, we may feel hesitant about speaking up in class, to share our thoughts. But once we learn the tools, the result is liberating. We want to go into the deep end of thinking. We want to dive in. We want to touch the bottom, to explore. This comparison seems to resonate with young people, and they become excited to learn the tools so that they can go in the "deep end" of thinking.

Headings below represent an outline of this chapter. Each section should accommodate different teaching styles or students' age-appropriate needs. One or more options may suit you.

Option 1: One Tool at a Time

Some teachers prefer a step-by-step approach, perhaps introducing one tool each day or week. The "One Tool at a Time" portion of this chapter should provide a welcome structure. Each tool features a picture idea, sample questions for teachers, and one or more sentence starters for students. Of course you choose your own pictures for in-class practice. I recommend 2–4 pictures per tool.

Option 2: All Tools at Once

Other teachers prefer a collective approach. A picture-slideshow of The 12 Tools may accomplish this preference. Each picture or series of pictures will demonstrate a specific tool. Students respond to the picture using a complete sentence, preferably restating the teacher's question as part of their declarative response. (These responses will later become **claims** or **topic sentences** for paragraph writing.) Following each picture slide is a "sentence starter" slide matching the teacher's question. Ideally, a student helper at the computer switches from picture to sentence starter, back and forth, at the teacher's prompting, allowing for students to respond. This method helps students practice their listening and response skills. As is common, many students are shy or hesitant to participate at first. However, projecting a picture seems to be a non-threatening way for students to learn the tools, and sentence-starters provide a means for even reluctant students to feel comfortable participating. Students (and teachers-in-training) clearly rely on them at first. I find students' minds want to dive in, even deeply, and sentence starters give them confidence to make the attempt.

Option 3: One-Page Tool Sheets: The 12 Tools

Finally, for teachers who just want the nuts and bolts—or who are time-depleted because of their already rigorous curriculum, the one-page tool sheets are really helpful. My students use them to enhance their papers by jumping from tool to tool, "stacking" their analyses as we will see demonstrated later. A digital copy of this book will allow for projecting a color version of the tools onto the wall for students to see. Full-color copies of select tools are available on the publisher's website. It's really nice when students can use the instrument right at their desk to improve their responses. And color reinforces their memory of each tool. Critical Thinking FRAMES (found after the one-page tool sheets) demonstrate how one might integrate tools when examining a single picture or text.

One Tool at a Time

#1 See, Don't See

A good detective can look at a crime scene and identify the clues by noticing the details of what he or she sees. A better detective will also notice what's *not* there. In fact, what is missing from a scene may in some cases be even more informative.

- **Project** a picture onto the board:

> **Picture ideas:**
>
> Cafeteria lunch
> Person being punished
> Driving a fancy car
> Olympian
> Person playing the piano
> Standing ovation
> Winning a sporting event
> Graduation

- **Teacher** asks something like this:
  - *What do you see? What do you **not** see?*
  - *What seems to be missing in _____?*
- **Sentence starter** (on the board):

What I see is/are _____, but what I don't see is/are _____ (likely) because _____.

↑ Evidence   ↑ Also Evidence   ↑ Rationale

#2 Change

Recognizing *explicit* change is really observation (knowledge); recognizing *implicit* change is really interpretation (comprehension). A good analyst notices both types of change, very often in nouns. *People, places, things, and ideas* have a way of developing or degenerating over time. And when something seemingly doesn't change, it may be equally significant. Being able to identify change in text is a good first step toward understanding how and why those changes occurred.

- ◆ **Project** a picture onto the board:

> **Picture ideas:**
>
> Caterpillar
> Superhero
> House being constructed
> Erosion, Pollution
> Pinocchio
> Baby learning to walk
> Character in a movie
> Grand Canyon

- ◆ **Teacher asks:** How does _____ change (over time)?
- ◆ **Student** replies with: _____ changes (by) _____.

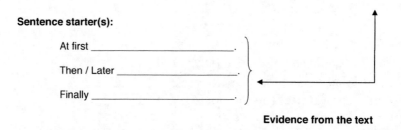

Sentence starter(s):

At first _____.

Then / Later _____.

Finally _____.

Evidence from the text

Please note: *Change* happens with respect to time, and a picture is a snapshot in time. Students will need to see changes *before* and *after* the moment in the picture. Change, we also know, may be understood as a series of causes and effects (see Tool #5) over time, reminding us The 12 Tools regularly coincide.

#3 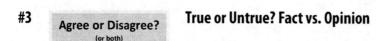 True or Untrue? Fact vs. Opinion

Foundational to higher-level thinking is determining whether to agree or disagree (or some combination of both). Implied in this decision is to determine whether something is true or not.

Figure 2.1

Thumbs up		⬤ Green Light = Agree
OR	OR	◯ Yellow Light = Unsure/Both
Thumbs down		⬤ Red Light = Disagree

- **Teacher asks:** *Do you agree or disagree with* _____?
- **Optional:** Students give a "Thumbs up or Thumbs down" sign, depending on whether they agree or disagree, respectively; or they hold up a small colored circle (possibly laminated) that indicates their points of view. In this way, a teacher can immediately check for understanding.
- **Project** a picture onto the board:

> **Picture ideas:**
>
> Student looking on neighbor's paper
> Basketball player fouling
> Bullying
> Riding a motorcycle
> Texting during class
> School uniforms
> Girl on boys' team

- **Teacher asks:** Do you agree or disagree with _____? Why? Is this a fact or opinion? Why?
- **Sentence starter(s):**
   - I agree/disagree with _____ because _____.
   - I both agree and disagree with _____ because_____.
   - I might agree with the _____ if _____.
   - When _____ says _____, it is an opinion/fact because _____.
      (The strength of the opinion is evaluation.)
                                                         ↑
                                          Evidence or rationale

#4   **Says This, Means That**   **(Symbols, Figurative Language, &**
          Figurative Language Symbol Inference   **Inference)**

Optional visual aid: It is imperative students understand different instances when a text will say one thing but mean another. For younger grades, the following double-sided signs could be easily utilized as a visual to teach

Figure 2.2

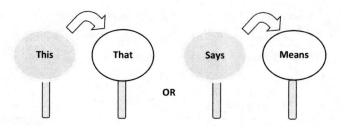

symbols, figurative language, and inferences, which all say one thing and mean another.

Symbol

- **Project** a picture onto the board:

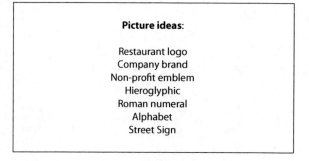

- **Teacher asks:** When the photographer/artist uses _____, what might it symbolize (or mean)?
    - **Sentence starter:** When the artist uses a ____, it might symbolize _____ because _____.
                                                                  ↑   ↑
                                                      Rationale   Evidence

Figurative Language

- **Project** a picture onto the board:

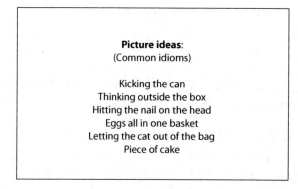

- **Teacher asks**: When the photographer shows _____, what might she/he really be saying?
- **Sentence starter:** *When the photographer shows _____, what she/he might really be saying is ____ because____.*

Inference
- **Project** a picture onto the board:

> **Picture ideas:**
>
> Satirical cartoon
> People in line for food
> Angry coach
> Protestors
> Fireworks
> Person crying

- **Teacher asks**: When the cartoonist uses a picture of a ____, what might he/she really be saying?
- **Sentence Starter:** When the cartoonist uses a ____, he/she might really be saying _____.

#5 Make a List (Analysis: Close Reading, Itemizing)
Close Reading   Itemizing

To appreciate the whole, one must understand the parts. **Close reading** asks students to identify and label various parts or pieces of a given text in order to find or enhance meaning. Common practice invites students to mark the text in a variety of ways including underlines, asterisks, boxes, circles, arrows, punctuation marks, multicolored highlights, inscriptions, and other markings to deconstruct—or better, to disassemble—the text. In the past *deconstruction* has meant to take something apart to such a degree that it can virtually destroy meaning; the term *disassemble* might more accurately reflect our goal as teachers—to take something apart to *discover* meaning, thereby increasing our value of the whole. When we read something closely, we are essentially making a list. *Close reading* is one form (see also Chapter 7), and *itemizing* elements is another. At times it's easier to have students mark on the picture or text, and at other times it's easier to make a separate list.

♦ **Project** or distribute a picture:

Picture ideas:

A busy street or intersection
Carnival
Crowded restaurant
Birthday party
Classroom full of students
Sports crowd

Close Reading
- ♦ **Teacher** asks:
  - Using the close reading key I have provided, I need a volunteer to identify and label _____ in the picture on the board.
  - Using the close reading key I have provided, identify and label _____ in the picture you have in front of you.

Itemizing
  - List what you see (or don't see), hear (or don't hear), smell (or don't smell), etc.
  - Let's list _____ (e.g., persons, places, things, events, or ideas).
  - Rotate pictures when the time is up, and we'll list _____.

#6 Find a Link (Analysis: Making Connections)

Finding potential links—or connections—is a form of analysis. Basic choices include:

1) find similarities (compare)
2) find differences (contrast)
3) find patterns (correlation)
4) find possible causes
5) find possible effects

Map Note: The moment you choose to support a theory about a similarity, difference, pattern, cause, or effect, you have crossed the bridge from analysis to creation.

Link: Compare-Contrast

T-charts and Venn diagrams serve for regular compare-contrast exercises in many classes. For added depth, consider having students identify the type of similarity or difference. Possibilities include:

- symbolic, graphic
- social, environmental
- religious, spiritual
- cultural, geographic
- economic, professional
- behavioral
- physical, temporal, scientific
- mental, educational, ideological
- ethical, moral, legal
- consequential

♦ **Project** a picture onto the board:

> **Picture ideas:**
>
> State funeral procession
> Baptism, wedding
> Unemployment line
> Political rally
> Quinciñera, Bar Mitzvah
> Sports fans
> Cyclone

♦ **Teacher asks:**
  - What is the relationship between _____ and _____?
  - What connects these two _____?
  - How are _____ and _____ the same (or different)?

♦ **Sentence starter(s):**
  - One connection I see is between ____ and _____ and is ____ (likely because ___).
  - I see a _____ connection between _____ and _____ in the way that _____.
  - I see a _____ relationship between _____ and _____ in the way that _____.
  - _____ and _____ are the same/different in the way that they _____.

Link: Cause and Effect

While we are reading something in class, we may pause to label possible causes and effects of a given event. Drawing dots (in separate colors if possible) simplify a seemingly difficult task—and demonstrate relationships between causes and effects, as configurations below indicate:

Figure 2.3 Cause and Effect

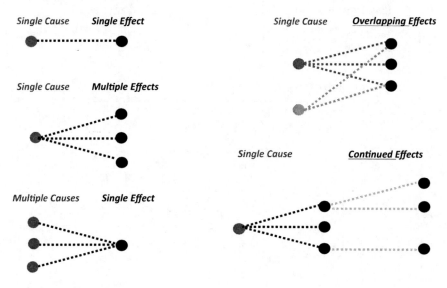

- ◆ **Teacher asks**:
  - Let's make a list of possible causes (or effects).
  - What (may have) caused _____? Why?
  - How will _____ affect _____?
- ◆ **Sentence starter(s)**:
  - What I think caused _____ is _____ because _____.
  - I think _____ will affect _____ by _____.
  - What I think will be the effect of _____ is _____.
  - Potential/continuing effects may include _____.

Please note: *Causes were once effects*. Our little diagrams are really "snapshots" in time. Also, as illustrated above, causes and effects can *overlap* and *continue* in their influence, forming virtually limitless configurations depending on the variables. Analysis by itself is neutral; a few questions above invite Creation.

- **Project** a picture onto the board:

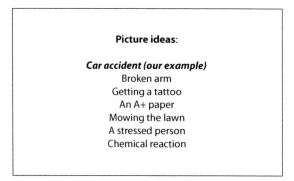

- **Teacher asks**: What are possible causes the car accident? **Possibly followed by**: Which one(s) does the evidence support?

Figure 2.4

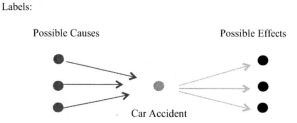

- **Sentence starter:** One possible cause of this *car accident* is _____.
  OR Possible causes for (or effects of) this *car accident* include:

  1. _____
  2. _____
  3. _____
  4. _____

  • The evidence supports the idea that _____ because _____.
  　　　　　　　　　　　　　　　　　　　↑　　　　　　　　↑
  　　　　　　　　　　　　　　　　　Claim　　　　　Evidence

Link: Correlation

As correlation seems to be the hardest for students, I will use a picture for demonstration. But first, an imperfect analogy: Correlation is a little like "fool's gold"—it looks a lot like cause-and-effect "gold" but isn't. News reporters and commentators regularly insinuate one thing is causing another—but really what they have found is a correlation—a pattern. Distinguishing between the two is the trick.

Consider the following example: Madison often falls asleep in her math class on Wednesdays. The math class (cause) appears to make her tired (effect). Clearly there is a correlation between Wednesday's math class and sleeping. The real cause, however, is likely her late-night dance practices on Tuesday evenings.

- ◆ **Project** a picture onto the board:

Figure 2.5

Photo by Jessica Taylor

- ◆ **Teacher explains**: Madison often falls asleep in her math class on Wednesdays (and only on Wednesdays). **Teacher asks**: So, what is the correlation (a pattern)—between what and what?
- ◆ **Sentence starter:**
    - I see a possible correlation (a pattern/trend) between _A_ and _B_.

Answer: —between *math class* and *sleeping*. This appears to be cause and effect (gold) but is really correlation (fool's gold).

- ◆ **Teacher explains:** Without more information, false conclusions might be made, like: "Math bores Madison" or "She is a bad math student" or "Wednesdays make her tired." Madison actually has a late-night dance class on Tuesdays, the real "cause and effect" (gold)—though evidence of this is not available in the picture.

Links Review

For clarification or review, consider drawing or displaying the following "links" one at a time. Remember, A and B can be virtually anything. The first three connections are pretty simple. The fourth, *correlation*, can be simple, too, if explained in relatable ways. Remind students of Madison sleeping in class: If "A" is Wednesday's math class and "B" is Madison falling asleep, then when "A" appears, "B" also appears. With no clear indication of why she is falling asleep, we only see a "pattern," but cannot ascertain if it is cause and effect. Another example: Students have noticed that when students' grades increase, more parents attend parent-teacher conferences. It may not be the grades causing the increased attendance.

Draw on the Board:

Figure 2.6 Draw on the Board

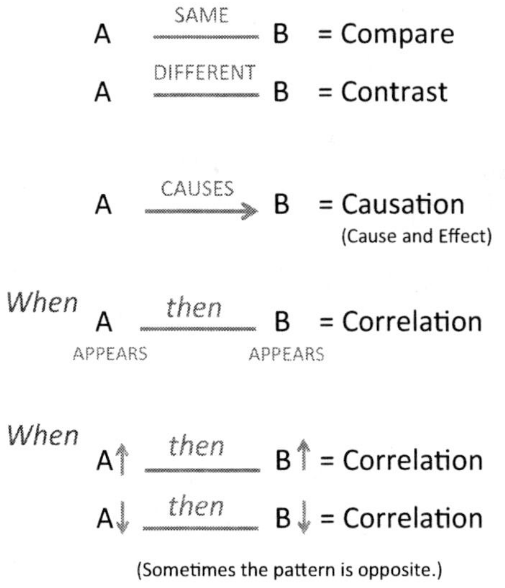

A ——SAME—— B = Compare

A ——DIFFERENT—— B = Contrast

A ——CAUSES→ B = Causation (Cause and Effect)

When A ——then—— B = Correlation
APPEARS   APPEARS

When A↑ ——then—— B↑ = Correlation

A↓ ——then—— B↓ = Correlation

(Sometimes the pattern is opposite.)

#7 If...., then.... **(conditional or hypothetical)**
    Future Present Past

Conditional or hypothetical claims are usually made in three ways: to predict (think *future*), to conclude (think *present*, or what something means), and to deduce (think *past*, or logic moving from one conclusion to another). The stair step reinforces the analogy of going deeper into the thinking pool. Also, if a teacher was to walk across the room, indicating the "If A" and "then B," "If B" and "then C" with hand gestures or pauses, it can provide another teacher visual to make this tool easy and fun.

- ◆ **Teacher draws** stairs on the board.

Figure 2.7

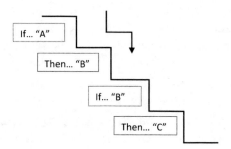

- ◆ **Project** a picture onto the board:

Figure 2.8

Art by Brandt Woods

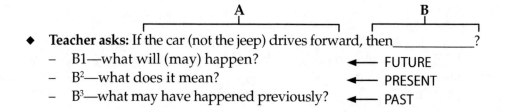

- ◆ **Teacher asks:** If the car (not the jeep) drives forward, then _____?
  - B^1—what will (may) happen? ← FUTURE
  - B^2—what does it mean? ← PRESENT
  - B^3—what may have happened previously? ← PAST

- **Sentence starter(s):**
  - If __"A"__, then __"B"__ must be true/will happen.
  - If __"A"__, then __"B"__ must be true/have happened.

Possible Exchange

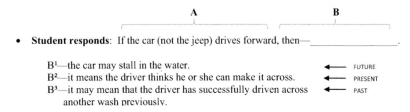

- **Student responds:** If the car (not the jeep) drives forward, then—_____.

    B¹—the car may stall in the water. ← FUTURE
    B²—it means the driver thinks he or she can make it across. ← PRESENT
    B³—it may mean that the driver has successfully driven across ← PAST
    another wash previously.

- **Teacher prompts further:**

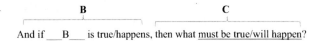

    And if __B__ is true/happens, then what <u>must be true/will happen</u>?

- **Student continues** deeper:

    B¹, C¹—If the engine stalls, then the driver may need to be rescued. ← FUTURE
    B², C²—If the driver thinks he can make it across, then it may mean ← PRESENT
    the driver is brave or foolish.
    B³, C³—If the driver has been successful crossing washes prior to this, ← PAST
    it may indicate a pattern of bold decisions in other previous behaviors.

Notes

Students may continue down the stairs, so to speak. In fact, forecasters and analysts will often make predictions several levels down. But obviously the more steps we continue down the stairs, the potentially farther away from evidence we go—and our conclusions can become precarious.

We want students to "go deep," so give them a little latitude when making predictions, conclusions, or deductions (even if they're a little unrealistic at first). Challenge them, of course, but let them explore. At the same time, teach them that auxiliary verbs like *may* or *might* can help ground their speculations. Adverbials like *possibly*, *likely*, *potentially*, or *conceivably* serve as hedges that can actually strengthen their responses because they're more likely to be accurate. Expressions like "It seems . . ." or "It appears . . ." or "This suggests . . ." are also helpful. Sometimes the phrase "Depending on . . ." may replace an "If" clause or phrase. Tool #7 naturally lends itself to cause-and-effect-like expressions—indeed many tools seem to overlap, naturally enhancing fluidity in paragraphs later.

#8 **Should – Would – Could** (Offering Alternatives)

One of the simplest tools is Tool #8, Should–Would–Could, and the three-word rhyme makes it easy for students to remember. On the Critical Thinking Map, "should" is a recommendation, which is a sort of bridge between evaluation and creation; "would" means either making a prediction or offering speculation, both forms of creation (because you are proposing a theory); and "could" is also speculation, again creation. In short, I tell students that if they use a "should, would, or could" to elaborate, it normally improves their responses (assuming, of course, that it relates to the topic or claim).

- ◆ **Project** a picture onto the board:

> **Picture ideas:**
>
> Runner fallen in a race
> Riding a bike in traffic
> Nearing white water
> Sneaking a cookie
> Late to class
> Homework vs. TV

- ◆ **Teacher asks** some form of these questions:
    - What should ____ do? What should be done?
    - What would ____ do? What would happen if ____?
    - What could ____ do? What can be done?
    - What should've/would've/could've been done instead/differently?
- ◆ **Sentence Starter(s):**
    - I believe ____ should/should have ____ *because* ____.
    - ____ should ____ because ____.
    - In order to ____, ____ should ____.
    - ____ would likely ____ because ____.
    - ____ could ____ in order to ____.
    - ____ should've/would've/could've ____ instead/differently. This would have ____.

#9 **Another's Point of View** (Perspective, Empathy)

- **Project** a picture onto the board:

> **Picture ideas:**
>
> Students in developing country
> Elderly in nursing home
> Child picked last for team
> Abuse victim
> Civil rights scene
> Food kitchen

- **Teacher asks** some form of one of these questions:
  - How might _____ (feel, believe, want) in this situation?
  - If you were _____ in this situation, how would you be feeling?
  - How might _____ view this situation compared to _____?
- **Sentence Starter(s):**
  - _____ (likely) feels _____ because _____.
  - _____ probably believe(s)/want(s) _____ because _____.

Note: Teach students to restate (or reference) other students' comments both to demonstrate understanding and courtesy. Equally important is the clarification that understanding how someone feels does not mean one has to agree with their point of view. The adage says, "Everyone has a right to an opinion, but not all opinions are right." And sometimes, both opinions are wrong. The goal of critical thinking is a search for truth insofar as evidence and reasoning can provide it. Proper empathy protects the conversation.

#10 **Application** (Use, Recycle, Transfer Use of, Personalize)

- **Project** a picture onto the board:

> **Picture ideas:**
>
> Cell phone as class tool
> Stack of used car tires
> Photovoltaic panels
> Aluminum cans
> IPad App
> Phone watch

- **Teacher asks** some form of one of these questions:
  - How can we apply _____ to _____ (at home, at work, at school, at play)?
  - Is it possible to take _____ and use (reuse) it _____?
  - How does _____ apply to your life (at home, at work, at school, at play)?
- **Student** replies using a complete sentence, something like:
  - We (can/cannot) apply _____ to our situation because _____.
  - We (can/cannot) use _____ because _____.
  - _____ (applies/does not apply) to _____ because _____.

↑ Evidence or a rationale

#11 Effective / Ineffective (evaluation: intent vs. result)

Evaluative Tool #7 has two parts: "Effective/Ineffective" (intent vs. result) and "Better or Worse" (using scale to construct a prediction).

- **Project** a picture onto the board:

  Picture ideas:

  Traffic signs
  Classifieds
  Company logo
  Billboard
  Chart or graph
  Diagram

- **Teacher asks** some form of one of these questions:
  - Is/Was _____ effective or ineffective (at _____)?
  - How effective or ineffective was _____ at _____?
  - How could _____ be more effective at _____?
- **Sentence Starter:**
  - _____ is/was effective/ineffective (at _____) because _____.
  - _____ would/could be more effective (at _____) if _____.

Better or Worse? (Evaluation: By Degree)

Younger students may benefit from having some sort of scale with which they may evaluate a given condition (or text). One can easily be created with a simple pattern. A normal sheet of 8.5" x 11" cardstock should produce three (thermometer-like) scales. For each line on the scale, write modifiers to suit your students' grade level (e.g., *a little, somewhat, considerably, significantly, a lot*). Obviously markers going up the scale will mirror markers going down. As long as the scale is designed "by degree," it should work. A paperclip works well as a slider, and laminating the scale protects it for future use. For each question, students adjust their scales and then hold up or compare their responses.

Figure 2.9 Optional Scales

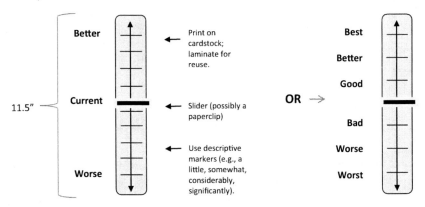

- ◆ **Project** a picture onto the board:

- **Teacher asks** some form of one of these questions:
    - Would _____ make it (the situation) better or worse?
    - How much better or worse? Why?
    - Let's make a rubric (or grading scale) that ranks, grades, assesses _____.
- **Optional:** Teacher then asks students to move the slider on the scale. Discussion follows.
- **Sentence Starter:**
    - I think ____ will be (a little/somewhat/considerably/significantly) (better/worse) if _____ because _____.

#12 Ranking (Evaluation: Prioritizing or Assessing)

This exercise is meant to be an evaluation, *not* a comparison. Compare-contrast invites students to think "same" or "different." But evaluation weighs why one is better than another: think "prioritizing" or a "ranking" (often by degree) of two or more items.

- **Preparation:** Small (optional) placards labeled A-D (possibly on different-colored, 8.5" x 11" cardstock and laminated for reuse) allow a teacher regularly to assign choices to each letter when examining text (e.g., author's ideas, evidences, choices, predictions, characters, methods, etc.). A teacher could invite a student to come up to the board (or small groups at their desks) and arrange the letters according to a given value or priority. Then invite them to explain their reasoning.

Practice: Rank these in order of confidence:

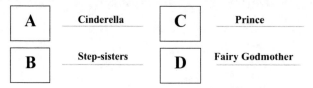

- **Project** fours picture onto the board, preferably at the same time, labeled A–D, respectively.

"Place these afternoon activities in order of priority."

A = Child doing homework	B = Child doing chores
C = Child eating a snack	D = Child playing

- **Teacher asks** some form of these questions:
    - Rank (prioritize or make a rubric of) these _____ based on _____.

  Validity   Importance   Efficiency   Difficulty
  Reliability Quality   Effectiveness   Cost, etc.

    - Is _____ or _____ better? Why? Why is _____ the best/worst?
    - Which answer best supports the idea that _____?
    - Let's make a rubric (or grading scale) that ranks, grades, assesses _____.
    - How can we test for accuracy? To make sure it's right? (validity)
    - How can we test for consistency? Or to make sure it's reliable?
- **Sentence starter(s):**
    - If I was to rank/prioritize these ____ according to [attribute], I would order them ____, ____, ____, ____ because ____.
    - I place ____ first (or consider ____ the best choice) because ____.
    - ____ is the most ____ (best example of ____) because ____.
    - ____ is better (____-er) than ____ because ____.
    - ____ should be the next choice because____. (continue)
    - ____ should be placed last because _____.

Sometimes lower-ranked items may be recognized for qualities that higher-ranked items do not have. Teach students how to use phrases like, "Even though B should be ranked lower generally, it also possesses an attribute that might rank it higher under certain circumstances . . . " Or, "Granted, B is not as strong in ____, but could rank higher if ____." (Again students must use evidence or rationale to defend their ranking.) Standardized tests often employ this method, asking for the "best" answer.

- ◆ **Additional development:** Teachers regularly use rubrics in their classroom to assess students' work. Consider the value of having students create a basic rubric to assess the text they are studying. It will teach them the nature of evaluation. Students will benefit from identifying both the qualities (to the left) and descriptions (inside the boxes). An example follows, Figure 2.11.

Figure 2.10 Rubric: Identifying Qualities

	4	3	2	1
Quality #1				
Quality #2				
Quality #3				
Quality #4				

All Tools at Once

A picture slideshow works really well to teach (or practice) The 12 Tools all at once (or over a few days). The goal is to help you create your own. After all, you will want the pictures you choose to be age and content specific.

How many practice pictures should a teacher use for each tool? I usually recommend 2–4 pictures, unless you intend to focus deeply on one tool. For example, my wife, who is also an English teacher, uses a 20+-slide presentation for Tool #11, Effective-Ineffective, featuring many street signs, billboards, advertisements, and other nonfiction visual texts to examine. Students love it. It's possible too few pictures may prevent really learning the tool, whereas too many pictures might bore students.

If you recall, following each "picture" slide is a "sentence starter" slide to which you (or your helper) will switch back and forth, allowing students to feel comfortable responding to the picture.

Figure 2.11 Evaluation: Validity & Reliability of a Text

Name: _____

Evaluation: Validity & Reliability of a Text
(accuracy)　　(consistency)

How valid is author's [claim, argument, evidence] that _____?

TRUSTING THE WHO
(Author or Source)

	4	3	2	1	
Credentials	Strong academic credentials	Good academic credentials	Fair academic credentials	Weak academic credentials	_____
Experience	Strong experience	Good experience	Fair experience	Weak experience	_____
Objectives (& Personal Biases)	Stated and Explained	Stated	Inferred	Withheld	_____
Peer Assessment	Strong Opinion	Good Opinion	Fair Opinion	Weak Opinion	_____

TRUSTING THE WHAT
(Claim Aligned with Evidence)

	4	3	2	1	
Claim(s) Given	Stated Specifically	Stated Generally	Stated Unclearly	Not Stated	_____
Facts and Opinions	Well-researched, Peer-reviewed	Good, possibly too general	At times off topic, unnecessary, biased	Missing, clearly biased, off topic	_____
Consistency (Repeated or Triangulated)	Results are Very consistent	Results are Generally consistent	Results are Seldom consistent	Results are Inconsistent	_____
Primary vs Secondary	Strong primary, Some secondary	Strong secondary, some primary	Some secondary, No primary	No primary, No secondary	_____

TRUSTING THE HOW
(*The Instrument* used to gather data or *Medium* used to present it)

	4	3	2	1	
Suits Audience	Best choice for gathering, presenting	Good choice for gathering, presenting	Seldom suits the audience	Does not suit the audience	_____
Unbiased	No biases in design	Few Biases, Minimal impact	Few Biases, Impactful	Fully-biased Design	_____
Organization	Clear, logical Structure or approach	Acceptable Structure or approach	Potentially Confusing Structure or approach	Missing Structure or approach	_____
Content	Tasks strongly match objective	Tasks generally match objective	Tasks rarely match objective	Tasks do not match objective	_____

Strong = 36 – 48　　Average = 24 – 36　　Poor = Under 24　　**TOTAL** _____

Here are sample tandem pairs of picture- and sentence-starter slides:

Tool #1: See, Don't See

Figure 2.12 Tool #1: See, Don't See

Photo by Jessica Taylor

Good answer: What I see is an older boy teasing a younger boy, but what I don't see is the reason why.

Good answer: What I see is an older boy teasing a younger boy, but what I don't see are adults (parents or teachers) monitoring the situation.

Better answer: What I see is an older boy teasing a younger boy, but what I don't see are parents or teachers monitoring the situation, possibly because the boys are at home unsupervised or on the playground where a teacher can't intervene. It's also possible adults want the boys to work it out.

Tool #3: Agree or Disagree

Figure 2.13 Tool #3: Agree or Disagree

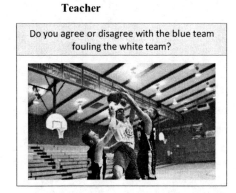 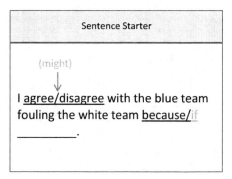

Photo by Jessica Taylor

Good answer: I disagree with the blue team fouling the white team because the player on the white team might get hurt. It's poor sportsmanship.

Good answer: I agree with the blue team's decision to foul the white team because it will prevent an easy lay-up and force the player to shoot two free throws at the line to earn his points.

Better answer: I *might* disagree with the blue team fouling the white team *if* either of the blue players was in foul trouble. Having a top player foul out could cause them to lose the game. Or, if a referee was to call a technical for a particularly rough foul, the white team would receive two shots for the technical *and* get the ball back. This would give the white team a significant advantage.

Tool #11: Effective-Ineffective

Figure 2.14 Tool #11: Effective/Ineffective

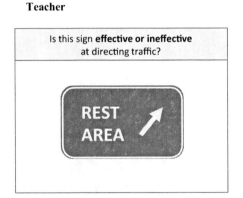

Photo by Clker.com

Good answer: This sign is effective at directing traffic because the sign is easy to read with the white letters on a dark background. The arrow helps the driver know which way to turn.

Better answer: This sign could be more effective if symbols were added to show the amenities available at the rest stop, like a bathroom, picnic table, or tent—or if it is handicap accessible.

Verbal responses such as these are very appropriate.

Tool Templates

For added practice and to check for understanding among all your students, consider using a Tool Template on which students write their responses before giving them aloud. Your template may vary slightly depending on your approach. If you want to practice a single tool using several pictures, your template might look something like this:

Figure 2.15 Tool Template

FRONT ONLY

TOOL BEING PRACTICED: _____

Picture #1: _____
_____
_____

Picture #2: _____
_____
_____

Picture #3: _____
_____
_____

Picture #4: _____
_____
_____

Picture #5: _____
_____
_____

Picture #6: _____
_____
_____

"Going Deep" into ONE TOOL:

Students use sentence-starter-slides to guide their complete sentences on the lines provided.

A few notes: If you are practicing Tool #5, "Lists and Links," only the *link* portion works well with the template above (e.g., "I see a ____ connection/relationship between ____ and ____ because ____."). To have students make a **list** that examines either the text or context, you may prefer Close Reading (what I used to call "Reading with a Pen,") or an alternative Tool Template (see Figure 3.6, page 63)—what you could collectively call an Analysis Packet. Also, when practicing Tool #11, "Effective-Ineffective," the second half of that tool is "Better or worse." I would recommend giving both halves equal practice.

Figure 2.16 Analyzing Text: Make a List

Name: _____

Analyzing Text: Make a List

Today we are going to analyze _____.
(the text)

Directions: Check a box. Then list examples from the text and/or mark on the text itself. Repeat.

What was said | How it was said

Ideas & Content
- [ ] Theme(s) or Ideas
- [ ] Arguments
- [ ] Events
- [ ] Persons
- [ ] Places
- [ ] Things
- [ ] Choices
- [ ] Changes
- [ ] Evidences
- [ ] Other: _____

Organization
- [ ] Beginning, Middle, End
- [ ] Plot
- [ ] Topical
- [ ] Chronological
- [ ] Sequential
- [ ] Cause & Effect
- [ ] Problem & Solution
- [ ] Compare & Contrast
- [ ] Outline
- [ ] Other: _____
- [ ] Medium*

Sentence Fluency
- [ ] Fragments
- [ ] Simple Sentences
- [ ] Complex Sentences
- [ ] Compound Sentences
- [ ] Compound-Complex
- [ ] Comma Splices
- [ ] Run-ons
- [ ] Phrases
- [ ] Clauses
- [ ] Other: _____

Word Choice
- [ ] Nouns
- [ ] Verbs
- [ ] Adjectives
- [ ] Adverbs
- [ ] Sensory words
- [ ] Technical words
- [ ] Dialect
- [ ] Slang
- [ ] Other: _____

Voice
- [ ] Funny
- [ ] Angry
- [ ] Matter-of-fact
- [ ] Sarcastic
- [ ] Cynical
- [ ] Innocent
- [ ] Scared
- [ ] Other: _____

Conventions
- [ ] Periods
- [ ] Question Marks
- [ ] Exclamation Points
- [ ] Commas
- [ ] Colons
- [ ] Semicolons
- [ ] Hyphens
- [ ] Dashes
- [ ] Parentheses
- [ ] Brackets
- [ ] Ellipses
- [ ] Quotation Marks

LIST A _____   LIST B _____   CLOSE READING

1. _____
2. _____
3. _____
4. _____
5. _____
6. _____
7. _____

Make two lists down or one list across. Use the back if necessary.

My text-marking key:

I have starred _____

I have underlined _____

I have highlighted _____

I have circled _____

I have boxed _____

I have _____

I have _____

*How (*Medium*)
- [ ] Speech
- [ ] Letter
- [ ] Article
- [ ] Graphic
- [ ] Essay
- [ ] Textbook
- [ ] Website
- [ ] Play
- [ ] Memoir
- [ ] Novel
- [ ] Book
- [ ] Diary
- [ ] Report
- [ ] Contract
- [ ] Declaration
- [ ] Treatise
- [ ] Movie, Script
- [ ] Short Story
- [ ] Conversation
- [ ] Academic Journal
- [ ] Text, E-mail
- [ ] Poem, Lyrics
- [ ] Social Media, Blog
- [ ] News Media
- [ ] Pamphlet
- [ ] Instructions
- [ ] Flyer
- [ ] Signage
- [ ] Warranty
- [ ] List, Glossary
- [ ] Application
- [ ] Other: _____

Device or figurative language used: "Line from the text":

1. _____   _____
2. _____   _____
3. _____   _____
4. _____   _____
5. _____   _____
6. _____   _____
7. _____   _____

Figure 2.17 Analyzing Text: Find a Link

Name: _____

Analyzing Text: Find a Link
LINK: Compare & Contrast

Today we are going to analyze _____.
(the text or texts)

Compare T-Chart

Add type of relationship or connection (see list below):

Contrast T-Chart*

Add type of relationship or connection (see list below):

Possible relationships/connections:	Symbolic	Cultural	Graphic	Spatial	Physical
	Legal	Religious	Spiritual	Geographic	Economic
	Academic	Social	Temporal (time)	Linguistic	Scientific
	Racial, Ethnic	Ethical	Structural	Ideological	Professional

LINK: Cause & Effect
(Be careful: Is it correlation?)
Use the back, if necessary, to add dots for continuing effects.

1.   Possible Causes   Possible Effects

Event _____

2.   Possible Causes   Possible Effects

Event _____

LINK: Correlation

3.   Describe the pattern that you see: _____

_____
_____

Figure 2.18 Analyzing Text (Find a Link): Cause and Effect

Name: _____

Analyzing Text (Find a Link): Cause and Effect

Directions: Create a "Cause and Effect" Web that centers on an important event in the story or article, represented by the dot in the center. Work backwards to find possible causes and forward to find possible effects, adding dots as necessary.

(EVENT)

Figure 2.19 Analyzing Text (Find a Link): Cause and Effect

Name: _____

Analyzing Text (Find a Link): Cause and Effect

Today we are going to analyze _____.
(the text)

Directions: Create a "Cause and Effect" web that centers on an important event in the story or article, represented by the center dot. Work backwards to find possible causes and forward to find possible effects, adding dots as necessary.

Possible Causes   **Possible Effects**

- Teachers spend class time checking clothing
- Popularity in clothing
- Gang-related tensions
- Violence at school
- Large gap economically
- Cliques forming on campus

- Too many distractions
- Safety concerns
- Social inequality a problem

New Uniform Policy (EVENT)

- Fewer Distractions
  - Increased classroom focus
  - Increased enjoyment
- Crime may decrease
  - Students feel safer
  - Enrollment may go up
- New wardrobe needed
  - Some parents upset
  - Fundraisers may be needed

SAMPLE: After reading an article on the requiring uniforms at school, students explore the possible causes and effects of such a policy decision.

40 ◆ The 12 Tools

Figure 2.20 Analyzing Context

Name: _____

Analyzing Context

We are going to analyze **the context** of _____.

(text or source)

Who (wrote it or spoke it)

NAME(S): _____

Gender: ☐ Male   ☐ Female

Age (when he/she wrote the text): _____

Race or Ethnicity: _____

Education (when he/she wrote the text):
☐ Elementary   ☐ Technical School
☐ Middle School   ☐ Bachelor's Degree
☐ High School   ☐ Master's Degree
☐ Associates Degree ☐ Doctoral Degree

Describe person's occupation, expertise: _____
_____

Impetus or Inciting Event: _____

Relevant background information: _____
_____

To Whom (it was written or spoken)

Target AUDIENCE: _____

Gender: ☐ Male   ☐ Female   ☐ Both

Age: _____   Race or Ethnicity: _____

Relationship to the author(s): _____

Describe audience: _____
_____

Education (of audience): _____

Why this individual / group is listening or reading: _____
_____

Relationship to the author(s): _____

Relevant background information: _____

When (it was written or spoken)   ☐ Unknown

Day _____ Month _____ Year _____

If relevant, time of day _____ AM / PM

Fill in one or more blanks:

Before _____

After _____

As _____

When _____

While/During _____

Where (it was written or spoken)   ☐ Unknown

Location (city, state, country, event): _____

Source Name: _____

☐ Volume _____   ☐ Heading _____
☐ Page _____   ☐ Paragraph _____
☐ Section _____   ☐ Stanza, verse: _____

Why (it was written or spoken)—*author's purpose*

Check **all** that (may) apply: Fill in the blank:

Expository   ☐ to inform _____
               ☐ to teach _____
(Functional)   ☐ to transact / sell _____
               ☐ to _____
Persuasive   ☐ to persuade _____
               ☐ to argue _____
               ☐ to intimidate _____
               ☐ to advertise _____
               ☐ to _____
Expressive   ☐ to express feelings about _____
               ☐ to entertain _____
               ☐ to inspire _____
               ☐ to _____
Descriptive   ☐ to describe _____
Narrative   ☐ to tell a fictional/non-fictional story about
(Literary)   _____
               ☐ to _____

Figure 2.21 The Profiler

Name: _____

The Profiler

Create a profile of the author or character (or invent your own character).

NAME: _____	Education: _____	Work: _____
Gender: _____	Where: _____	Vehicle: _____
Age: _____	Body Shape: _____	Hobbies: _____
Race/Ethnicity: _____	Clothing: _____	_____
Height: _____ Weight: _____	_____	Weaknesses: _____
Hair Color: _____	_____	_____
Eye Color: _____	Shoes: _____	Strengths: _____
Skin Color: _____	Jewelry: _____	_____
Hang-out: _____	One past experience: _____	Close to: _____
Special Talent: _____	_____	Bothered by: _____
Hidden secret: _____	_____	Got into trouble once when: ___
_____	One past love: _____	_____
Idiosyncrasies: _____	_____	Friends: _____
_____	One hope of the future: _____	_____
Fears: _____	_____	_____
_____	Biases: _____	Enemy: _____
Religious belief: _____	Object always with the person:	What goes wrong for this person?
Clubs/ Memberships: _____	_____	_____
_____	Familiar phrase the person uses:	_____
What drives him/her: _____	_____	How does she or he try to escape
_____	_____	or fix the situation? _____
Wealth: _____	Parents' names: _____	_____
Favorites: _____	_____	_____
_____	_____	_____

When practicing **all of the tools at once,** a single picture may suffice for teaching a few different tools, four or five pictures for all 12 Tools. A Tool Template organizer might look something like this:

Figure 2.22 Tool Template (Front)

FRONT

TOOL PRACTICE

Tool #1: See, Don't See

Tool #2: Change

Tool #3: Agree or Disagree

Tool #4: Says This, Means That

Tool #5: Make a List (See also Figure 2.17)

Tool #6: Find a Link

Figure 2.23 Tool Template (Back)

BACK

Tool #7: If…, then…

Tool #8: Should-Would-Could

Tool #9: Another's Point of View

Tool #10: Application

Tool #11: Effective/Ineffective (Better or Worse)

Tool #12: Ranking

An important question arises: *How do I get my students to transition from pictures to text?* Try the same approach, only this time project textual excerpts instead of pictures. Modified templates (see Figure 2.24 for multiple excerpts or Figure 2.25 for multiple tools) provide space for similar, critical responses.

Figure 2.24 Modified Tool Template 1

FRONT (only)

TOOL PRACTICE

Tool #1: See, Don't See

Tool #2: Change

Tool #3: Agree or Disagree

Tool #4: Says This, Means That

Tool #5: Make a List (See also Figure 2.16)

Tool #6: Find a Link

"Going Deep" into ONE EXCERPT:

For this template, you might display one excerpt on the board and solicit multiple responses using multiple tools regarding it.

Figure 2.25 Modified Tool Template 2

Write a mini-quote or main idea of the excerpt here

TOOL BEING PRACTICED: _____

Excerpt #1: _____

Excerpt #2: _____

Excerpt #3: _____

Excerpt #4: _____

Excerpt #5: _____

Excerpt #6: _____

"Going Deep" into ONE TOOL:

For this template, you might extract multiple excerpts from a text, having students write all or a portion of the excerpt on the line provided. Students then use the same tool over and over again to write their responses.

Obviously textual slides will correspond to the text you are using in class. The number of tools you choose for each excerpt is up to you. For illustration, using the same three tools as before, here are a few sample slides this time featuring text. The teacher has her students examine Dumbledore's advice in J.K. Rowling's *Harry Potter and the Sorcerer's Stone*:

Tool #1: See, Don't See

Figure 2.26 Tool #1: See, Don't See

Teacher	Student
What do you see? What do you **not** see?	Sentence Starter
"There are all kinds of courage," said Dumbledore smiling. "It takes a great deal of bravery to stand up to our enemies, but just as much to stand up to our friends" (221).	What I see is ____, but what I don't see is _____. ↑ (possibly because)

Good answer: What I see is Dumbledore giving advice about courage. What I don't see is Dumbledore explaining the possible consequences of standing up to your friends.

Better answer: What I see is Dumbledore giving advice about courage. What I don't see is Dumbledore giving an example from his own life to illustrate how hard it was to stand up to a friend. It's possible such experiences are too painful to share.

Tool #3: Agree or Disagree

Figure 2.27 Tool #3: Agree or Disagree

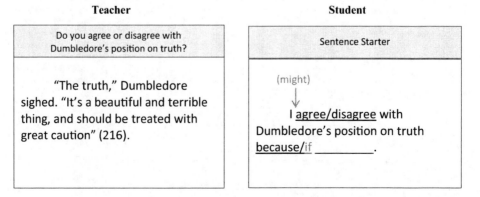

Good answer: I agree with Dumbledore's position because sharing truth can help someone who wants it, but it might also hurt someone who is not prepared for it.

Better answer: I both agree and disagree with Dumbledore's position on truth. I agree that sharing the truth can help *and* hurt, but it is certainly not terrible as he says. It's not truth that causes the pain itself, but how someone chooses to receive it.

Tool #11: Effective–Ineffective

Figure 2.28 Tool #11: Effective/Ineffective

Teacher	Student
Is Rowling affective or ineffective at creating a humorous tone?	Sentence Starter
"What happened down in the dungeons between you and Professor Quirrell is a complete secret, so, naturally the whole school knows."	Rowling is effective/ineffective at creating a humorous tone because _____.

Good answer: Rowling is effective at creating a humorous tone because she implies students are gossiping. Because we can relate, it's funny.

Better answer: Rowling is effective at creating a humorous tone because she implies students are gossiping at Hogwarts. Because we can relate, it's funny. Dumbledore **could** simply have said that the students at his school gossiped, but this **would** not have been as **effective** because it **would** have removed the discovery—and the humor for the reader.

This exercise of using a picture slide presentation to teach critical thinking tools has a way of livening up a class, and you may be surprised by the depth of some of their responses. At times what students say may not be grounded in evidence found within the picture. Two thoughts on this: one, conjecture is a form of exploration, and we want to encourage high-level examination, prompting us to allow wiggle room as they venture across the bridge toward a claim; and two, if students go too far, bring them back by asking if there is evidence in the picture (or text) to support their theory. Lack of evidence does not necessarily mean their speculations are wrong, only that they need more data. A student who arrives at the conclusion when more evidence is needed is making a remarkable step.

One-Page Tool Sheets: The 12 Tools

Coming up are one-page reference sheets entitled The 12 Tools, one version for teachers and another for students. I have also included a simplified (if overly general) Bloom's version providing a place for teachers to label their respective standards as they apply. When possible, I recommend color copies (check the publisher's website) as they seem to establish tool identity.

For teachers, a cursory glance at a One-page Tool Sheet may prompt discussion questions. A thorough review may inform potential writing prompts. Teachers have so little time; Question Starters—whether they are pulled from those found at the end of Chapter 1 or those on the One-page Tool Sheet—can help.

For students who are writing responses, Sentence Starters (1) **create topical claims** *before* the evidence is presented (potentially restating their teacher's question) or (2) **add depth to elaboration** *after* the evidence is presented within their responses. Chapters 5 and 7 demonstrate the latter application.

Thinking FRAMES

If you care to have students practice using their One-page Tool Sheets—which in essence is to practice critical thinking itself—consider using a Thinking FRAME. A frame consists of a series of boxes (one box per tool) around a center prompt: a picture, a text, a problem—anything. The idea is to have students use Sentence Starters from their One-page Tool Sheets to write one or more sentences in each box on the lines provided.

I see the goal of this type of exercise to demonstrate integration. The 12 Tools work together and are not as discrete as they may appear during their initial presentation. Often they dovetail each other, overlap, and even accomplish the same prediction or conclusion. But the tools do have nuanced approaches individually and may yet offer some unique insight otherwise unavailable.

Following the tool sheets, I first provide a blank Thinking FRAME template for teachers; you need only add the prompt. (I recommend starting with a picture as a scaffold to text.) I then provide three examples: a *picture* of two cheerleaders holding a poster, *an excerpt* of Robert Frost's poem "The Road Not Taken," and a student-centered social *problem*. Each example has a sample key. Please keep in mind, however, that answers will vary and may be even better than the ones provided. Hold students accountable. Take the time to make them earn their comments. If they get too far away from the picture or text, gently redirect them; not everything they write has to be physically shown in the picture, but there should be a rationale that connects them to the evidence.

A couple thoughts: Tool #2 is *Change*. Change occurs with respect to time, and a picture is really a snapshot in time. Change, then, is easier to identify in a story or article where something or someone morphs over time. Given the one-moment-in-time snapshot, this means that for the Thinking FRAME,

Figure 2.29 The 12 Tools (Teacher Version)

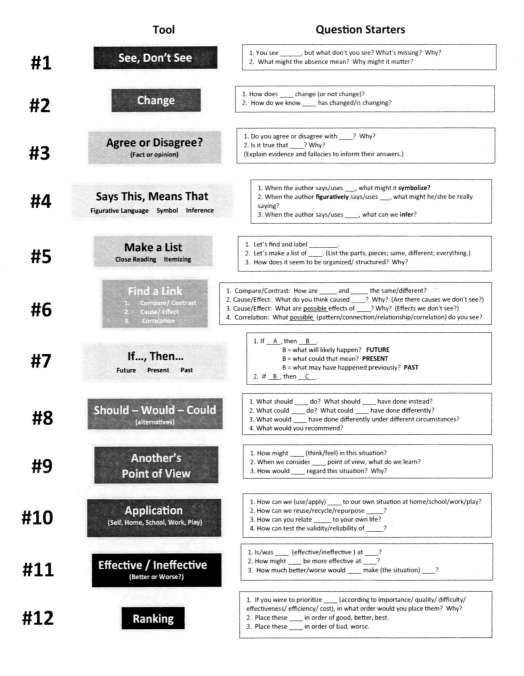

students are going to have to draw some inferences of what changed to arrive at the picture and what will likely change after picture. For Tool #5, *Make a List*, you may opt to close-read the text in lieu of or addition to making a list.

Figure 2.30 The 12 Tools (Student Version)

The 12 Tools
STUDENTS

	Tool	Sentence Starters
#1	**See, Don't See**	1. What I/we see is/are ___, but what I/we don't see is/are ___ (likely because ___). 2. The absence of ___ may mean ___.
#2	**Change**	1. At first, ___ was ___. 2. Then/Later ___ changed by (or did not change by) ___. 3. Finally/Toward the end, ___ (changed even more/returned to normal) by ___.
#3	**Agree or Disagree?** (Fact or opinion)	1. I agree/disagree with ___ because ___. 2. I might agree/disagree with ___ if ___. 3. When the author says ___, it's true/untrue because ___. 4. When the author says ___, it represents a fact/an opinion because ___.
#4	**Says This, Means That** Figurative Language Symbol Inference	1. When the author says/uses ___, it might it **symbolize** ___. 2. When the author **figuratively** says/uses ___, he/she might really be saying ___ 3. When the author says/uses ___, we can we **infer** ___.
#5	**Make a List** Close Reading Itemizing	1. I will find and label ___. (Close reading) 2. ___ seems to be organized/structured ___ in order to ___. 3. I will list ___. (List the parts, pieces; same, different; everything.)
#6	**Find a Link** 1: Compare/Contrast 2: Cause/Effect 3: Correlation	1. ___ and ___ are the same/different in ___. (Compare/Contrast) 2. What I think caused (or will cause) _A_ is _B_ because ___. (Cause/Effect) 3. One possible effect of ___ might/may/will include ___ because___. (Cause/Effect) 4. I see a possible [type] pattern/connection/relationship/correlation between _A_ or _B_ in the way ___. (Correlation)

#7	**If..., Then...**
	Future Present Past
		1. If _A_, then _B_.
		    B = then what will likely happen is ___. **FUTURE**
		    B = then what it means is ___. **PRESENT**
		    B = then what may have happened previously is ___. **PAST**
		2. If _B_, then _C_.

#8	**Should – Would – Could** (alternatives)	1. ___ should/should have ___ because ___. 2. If ___ would/would have ___, then ___. 3. ___ could ___. **OR** ___ could have ___.
#9	**Another's Point of View**	1. When I consider ___ point of view, I realize/we learn ___. 2. ___ may (think/feel) ___ because ___. 3. ___ might have (thought/felt) ___ because ___.
#10	**Application** (Self, Home, School, Work, Play)	1. (I/We) can (use/apply) ___ at home/school/work/play by/when ___. 2. We can reuse/recycle/repurpose ___ by/when ___. 3. I can relate to ___ because in my own life ___. 4. We can test the validity (accuracy)/reliability (consistency) of ___ by ___.
#11	**Effective / Ineffective** (Better or Worse?)	1. ___ is/was (effective/ineffective) at ___. 2. ___ might be more effective at ___ if ___. 3. ___ would make (the situation) better/worse (if/ because) ___.
#12	**Ranking**	Identify the choices first. Then prioritize them: 1. I would rank ___ in the following order ___, ___, ___, and ___. 2. _A_ is _[-er word]_ than _B_ because___. (continue ranking options) (faster, smarter, cheaper, stronger, better, more effective, etc.) 3. ___ is the best/worst ___ because ___.

See also Close Reading in Chapter 6. Tool #12 is *Ranking*. To engage this tool, students must identify alternatives to rank, which can be a little tricky if they don't see options at first (whether there are many or just a two). When students find alternatives, practice is possible.

Figure 2.31 The 12 Tools

The 12 Tools

Notes: 1) Tools naturally overlap; and 2) Students advance to Creation whenever a claim is attempted.

	Tool	Bloom's Taxonomy Level	Standard
#1	See, Don't See	KNOWLEDGE	
#2	Change	KNOWLEDGE (if change is explicit) COMPREHENSION (if change is implicit) CREATION (if a claim: prediction, etc.)	
#3	Agree or Disagree? (Fact or opinion)	COMPREHENSION CREATION (if a claim is created)	
#4	Says This, Means That Figurative Language Symbol Inference	COMPREHENSION	
#5	Make a List Close Reading Itemizing	ANALYSIS	
#6	Find a Link 1. Compare/Contrast 2. Cause/Effect 3. Correlation	ANALYSIS	
#7	If..., Then... Future Present Past	CREATION (conditional claim)	
#8	Should – Would – Could (alternatives)	CREATION (would, could) & EVALUATION (should)	
#9	Another's Point of View	CREATION (speculation)	
#10	Application (Self, Home, School, Work, Play)	APPLICATION	
#11	Effective / Ineffective (Better or Worse?)	EVALUATION & CREATION (recommendation)	
#12	Ranking	EVALUATION CREATION (claim)	

50 ◆ The 12 Tools

Figure 2.32 Thinking FRAME (Blank Template)

Thinking FRAME

Name: _____

1: See, Don't See

2. Change

3. Agree or Disagree
(Fact or opinion)

4. Says This, Means That
(Figurative Language, Symbol, Inference)

5. Make a List
My list of _____
- _____
- _____
- _____
- _____

AND/OR ☐ Close Reading

Examine the picture/text/problem below. Use **"The 12 Tools" Sentence Starters** to write critically about this prompt in the boxes provided.

6. Find a Link
(Compare, Contrast, Cause/Effect, Correlation)

7. If..., Then....
(Future, Present, Past)

8. Should-Would-Could

[Description of picture or text]

9. Another's Point of View

11. Effective / Ineffective
(Better or Worse)

10. Application
(Internalize, Use, Recycle, Repurpose)

12. Ranking

Figure 2.33 Thinking FRAME (Photo Analysis - Blank Template)

Thinking FRAME

Name: _____

1: See, Don't See

2. Change

3. Agree or Disagree
(Fact or opinion)

4. Says This, Means That
(Figurative Language, Symbol, Inference)

5. Make a List
My list of _____
- _____
- _____
- _____
- _____

AND/OR ☐ Close Reading

Examine the picture/text/problem below. Use **"The 12 Tools" Sentence Starters** to write critically about this prompt in the boxes provided.

6. Find a Link
(Compare, Contrast, Cause/Effect, Correlation)

7. If…, Then….
(Future, Present, Past)

Cheerleaders hold a sign before a football game.

8. Should-Would-Could

9. Another's Point of View

11. Effective / Ineffective
(Better or Worse)

10. Application
(Internalize, Use, Recycle, Repurpose)

12. Ranking

52 ◆ The 12 Tools

Figure 2.34 Thinking FRAME (Photo Analysis); Cheerleaders hold a sign before a football game.

KEY — Answers will vary

Thinking FRAME

Name: _____

1: See, Don't See

What I see are two cheerleaders holding a sign, but what I don't see is the rest of their squad. It's possible these two girls are the captains.

4. Says This, Means That
(Figurative Language, Symbol, Inference)

When the photographer shows a picture of a cowboy, it might symbolize their school's mascot. We can infer from their slogan that these girls support cancer research.

2. Change

At first, the paper was all white, probably on a roll. Then it became a sign when fans painted it. Later it was raised vertically. In the end it will likely be torn as football players run through it to start the game.

3. Agree or Disagree
(Fact or opinion)

When the author says "Go Pink or Go Home," it represents an opinion because they believe supporting breast cancer research is important.

5. Make a List

My list of a cheerleader's uniform items
- Long-sleeve shirts with logo
- Matching skirts
- Dark Socks, White shoes
- Hair ties

AND/OR ☐ Close Reading

Examine the picture/text/problem below. Use "The 12 Tools" Sentence Starters to write critically about this prompt in the boxes provided.

Cheerleaders hold a sign before a football game.

6. Find a Link
Compare, Contrast, Cause/Effect, Correlation
SAME   DIFFERENT

It appears that this sign was made by the girls. Possible causes for their effort include obedience to their instructor, love for their school, a desire to be noticed, and a goal to be unified as a team.

7. If..., Then....
(Future, Present, Past)

If they continue to hold the sign, then players will likely run through it (future). If they pose for pictures, it means they are proud of their work (present). If they are the ones holding it, then they may have made the sign (past).

8. Should-Would-Could

The young women should keep a copy of any pictures they take so they can remember the moment.

10. Application
(Self, Home, School, Work, Play)

I can apply a similar giving attitude in my own life by supporting causes that help others in need.

11. Effective / Ineffective
(Better or Worse)

These girls painted an effective sign because it supported two causes, their school and a charity. The sign could be somewhat better if it was to center the logo across the top, so they wouldn't have had to break up the word "home" into two pieces.

9. Another's Point of View

When I consider the parents' point of view, I realize they must feel proud of their daughters' efforts.

12. Ranking

I would plan the layout before beginning, getting a rough idea of size first to avoid mistakes. Then I would paint the logo across the top. And finally, I would paint the mascot. This would balance the poster.

The 12 Tools ◆ 53

Figure 2.35 Thinking FRAME (Text Analysis—Blank Template)

Thinking FRAME

Name: _____

1: See, Don't See	2. Change	3. Agree or Disagree *(Fact or opinion)*
4. Says This, Means That *(Figurative Language, Symbol, Inference)*		**5. Make a List** My list of _____ • _____ • _____ • _____ • _____ AND/OR ☐ Close Reading
6. Find a Link *(Compare, Contrast, Cause/Effect, Correlation)*		**7. If…, Then….** *(Future, Present, Past)*
8. Should-Would-Could	**11. Effective / Ineffective** *(Better or Worse)*	**9. Another's Point of View**
10. Application *(Self, Home, School, Work, Play)*		**12. Ranking**

Examine the picture/text/problem below. Use **"The 12 Tools"** Sentence Starters to write critically about this prompt in the boxes provided.

Excerpt from **"The Road Not Taken"**

1st Stanza
  Two roads diverged in a yellow wood,
  And sorry I could not travel both
  And be one traveler, long I stood
  And looked down one as far as I could
  To where it bent in the undergrowth…

4th Stanza
  I shall be telling this with a sigh
  Somewhere ages and ages hence:
  Two roads diverged in a wood, and I—
  I took the one less traveled by,
  And that has made all the difference.

By Robert Frost

Figure 2.36 Thinking FRAME (Text Analysis)

KEY — Answers will vary

Thinking FRAME

Name: _____

1: See, Don't See

What I see is a man traveling down a less-traveled path, but what I don't see is what the path represented in his own life.

2. Change

At first the man is regretful because he wants to take both paths. Then he seems studious, examining the details of both paths. Finally, he is grateful for having chosen the less-traveled path.

3. Agree or Disagree
(Fact or opinion)

I agree with Frost's decision to take the road less traveled because it means there are more chances to make discoveries unavailable to most people.

4. Says This, Means That
(Figurative Language, Symbol, Inference)

When Frost says "Two roads diverged in the yellow wood," he likely means that life has important decisions for us to make.

5. Make a List

My list of literary devices in the poem
- End rhyme & rhyme scheme
- Repetition
- Stanza
- Polysyndeton

AND/OR ☐ Close Reading

6. Find a Link
(Compare, Contrast, Cause/Effect, Correlation)

I see a correlation between the "yellow wood" and looking back. Yellow is a fall color, a season before winter when everything dies. Frost is looking back before he dies, remembering his decision.

Examine the picture/text/problem below. Use **"The 12 Tools" Sentence Starters** to write critically about this prompt in the boxes provided.

Excerpt from **"The Road Not Taken"**

1st Stanza
Two roads diverged in a yellow wood,
And sorry I could not travel both
And be one traveler, long I stood
And looked down one as far as I could
To where it bent in the undergrowth...

4th Stanza
I shall be telling this with a sigh
Somewhere ages and ages hence:
Two roads diverged in a wood, and I—
I took the one less traveled by,
And that has made all the difference.

By Robert Frost

7. If..., then....
(Future, Present, Past)

If he is grateful now looking back at his decision to take the road less traveled, then it means he also recognizes his immaturity or inexperience for being "sorry [he] could not travel both" (conclusion).

8. Should-Would-Could

He could have said "today" instead of "ages and ages hence." Maybe he doesn't see death as the end.

10. Application
(Self, Home, School, Work, Play)

I can apply Frost's decision to my own life. To make a difference in my education, I will have to take less-traveled paths, which means earning high grades.

11. Effective / Ineffective
(Better or Worse)

Frost effectively uses imagery in the poem. Readers can picture a path leading in two directions in a forest, possibly with yellow leaves everywhere. The poem might be a little better if he used additional images.

9. Another's Point of View

When I look through the eyes of those who took the common road, I might look back and feel sad that I took an easier path where I didn't learn as much.

12. Ranking

The most important device Frost uses is imagery, creating a picture. Next is polysyndeton, using "and" to start three separate lines, making it easier to read. Repetition is last but helps with meter.

Figure 2.37 Thinking FRAME (Problem Analysis—Blank Template)

Thinking FRAME

Name: _____

| 1: See, Don't See | 2. Change | 3. Agree or Disagree (Fact or opinion) |

4. Says This, Means That
(Figurative Language, Symbol, Inference)

5. Make a List
My list of _____

- _____
- _____
- _____

AND/OR ☐ Close Reading

Examine the picture/text/problem below. Use **"The 12 Tools" Sentence Starters** to write critically about this prompt in the boxes provided.

    Jacob is a hardworking student. When he brings his science project to class, he proudly begins to set it up. He pulls out a screwdriver attached to his utility knife in his pocket and begins to fasten his display together. When the teacher sees it, she confiscates the instrument, reprimanding him for bringing a knife to school. She escorts him to the principal's office and writes a referral. The principal is sympathetic to Jacob's mistake but suspends him for 10 days from school, according to their school's "zero tolerance" policy. A hearing must now be held to determine if Jacob will be allowed to come back. Meanwhile, Jacob must make up work for assignments and will not be allowed to participate in the science fair.

6. Find a Link
(Compare, Contrast, Cause/Effect, Correlation)

7. If..., then....
(Future, Present, Past)

8. Should-Would-Could

9. Another's Point of View

11. Effective / Ineffective
(Better or Worse)

10. Application
(Self, Home, School, Work, Play)

12. Ranking

56 ◆ The 12 Tools

Figure 2.38 Thinking FRAME (Problem Analysis—Blank Template)

KEY — Answers will vary

Thinking FRAME

Name: _____

1: See, Don't See
What we see is Jacob's situation, but what we don't see is Jacob's reaction to his punishment.

2. Change
At first Jacob was probably excited about science because he completed his project "proudly". Then he was likely confused by his treatment, maybe causing him to mistrust his teacher and the school. In the end, he may not like science as much, if at all.

3. Agree or Disagree
(Fact or opinion)

I agree with the principal's decision to enforce the policy because rules are important. But I disagree with the policy. It should allow administrators an opportunity to make better decisions.

4. Says This, Means That
(Figurative Language, Symbol, Inference)

When the policy says "zero tolerance," it really means that authorities can no longer use their own judgment. They must punish no matter what.

5. Make a List
My list of disciplinary steps

- Confiscates utility knife
- Reprimands him
- Escorted to office
- Referral, Suspension, Hearing

AND/OR ☐ Close Reading

6. Find a Link
(Compare, Contrast, Cause/Effect, Correlation)

Possible causes for the policy might include previous violence or pressure from the community or other districts.

> Examine the picture/text/problem below. Use **"The 12 Tools" Sentence Starters** to write critically about this prompt in the boxes provided.
>
> Jacob is a hardworking student. When he brings his science project to class, he proudly begins to set it up. He pulls out a screwdriver attached to his utility knife in his pocket and begins to fasten his display together. When the teacher sees it, she confiscates the instrument, reprimanding him for bringing a knife to school. She escorts him to the principal's office and writes a referral. The principal is sympathetic to Jacob's mistake but suspends him for 10 days from school, according to their school's "zero tolerance" policy. A hearing must now be held to determine if Jacob will be allowed to come back. Meanwhile, Jacob must make up work for assignments and will not be allowed to participate in the science fair.

7. If..., then....
(Future, Present, Past)

If Jacob's teacher confiscates the utility knife, it means she follows rules (present).
If she is quick to reprimand her student, it may mean she has reprimanded students before (past).

8. Should-Would-Could
The school district should amend its policy to allow leaders to examine a situation to see if a punishment is even necessary.

11. Effective / Ineffective
(Better or Worse)

The principal might be more effective if he or she approached the schoolboard and asked for a better policy, one that protected all students—even ones who are trying to do the right thing.

9. Another's Point of View
Jacob's parents probably feel discouraged by their son's treatment because he was made an honest mistake but was trying to do his project.

10. Application
(Self, Home, School, Work, Play)

We can use Jacob's example in our own school by reexamining our "zero tolerance" policy. Maybe our principal should be allowed to decide what's best.

12. Ranking
The best solution would be to confiscate the instrument but then help Jacob finish setting up his project. The next would be to contact parents and explain the situation. The least appropriate is suspension.

3

The Evidence Finder

One day while roofing a house, I applied black tar paper in preparation for shingles that would go on top. For nearly an hour, I nailed down small orange wafers every few inches to keep the paper in place against the wind. For all my labor, I was only able to complete a small section of the roof. The process was tedious and long. Then my father drove up. He smiled and then proceeded to attach a power-tool to an air compressor. Once on the roof, he unceremoniously grinned, "Step aside, son." Bam, bam, bam, bam! As fast as he could move, my father used this gun-like mechanism to shoot those little orange wafers onto the roof. I watched in awe. In minutes he finished almost the entire project, minus my very humbling contribution, forever reminding me that I was still very much a student. Now, was there anything wrong with my hammer? No. A hammer is a good tool. But this lesson taught me one very important principle: the right tool—a better tool—can make a process a whole lot easier.

The Evidence Finder is one power-tool of reader responses. If I intend to have students respond to a text using evidence to support their answer, this is my instrument of choice. You are ready for this tool when you have a good reader-response question. Hopefully Question Starters in tandem with the Critical Thinking Map will enable you to write carefully targeted prompts. Keep in mind ordinary text-dependent questions require students to use a text to find an answer (think scavenger hunt), but *inferential* text-dependent questions invite deeper understanding and elaboration (think mining).

Getting Started

Once you have carefully designed a question, you are ready to ask students to find textual evidence in preparation for writing a paragraph. You have a choice to make: Do you want students to fill out an Evidence Finder as they read or after they've completed reading the text? For longer literary selections, I prefer to have students fill out their organizers while we read together, and not simply because I want to guide their practice in learning how to find and organize their evidence; teachers know that graphic organizers have a way of keeping students' attention. For shorter selections, I might help students complete an Evidence Finder afterwards, going back over the text as needed.

When you have read a literary selection or are ready to begin reading one, you may want to write the question you designed on the board. Next, give each student a copy of an Evidence Finder in front of them to complete. (A digital copy of this book provides user-friendly templates.) My favorite approach is to project a blank copy of an Evidence Finder onto a white (or smart) board. I see two advantages in projecting the document: first, I can tease out the best responses during class discussion and write them in the corresponding boxes for students to see, which responses students then replicate on their own organizers, an effective form of guided practice (and pacing); and second, I can use different-colored markers for each box. Colors have a way of helping students visually differentiate the pieces.

On the next page is basic framework for *one* piece of evidence (see Figure 3.1). Fill out each box one at a time with students. Each box represents a key function relative to gathering and (later) presenting evidence. I recommend starting with the topic (or claim), then the quote, followed by the context, explanation, and analysis. Sometimes more than one piece of evidence needs to be gathered before analysis can be completed. You will know when students understand the tool when they begin asking if they can use alternative examples or wording, which is very appropriate if they have demonstrated proficiency first. Prepare students by asking:

Figure 3.1 What do you want to find?

I want to find evidence of _____ (This line focuses students' attention on what they will be looking for based on the teacher's question.)

Or CLAIM | Or ELABORATE

#	TOPIC	CONTEXT		QUOTE	EXPLAIN THE QUOTE	ANALYSIS
1		WHO	TO WHOM			
		WHEN	WHERE			

Topic (Example or Claim): Begin by helping students determine the topic or example. One word, or no more than a few words, should suffice when filling in the box with either the topic or claim. Keep it simple. Teach students that the topic of an informative paragraph on apples would simply be *apples* or *red delicious apples*; or for text-dependent questions, the topic would be the example from the text (explicit or implicit) that answers the question. If the statement is a prediction, conclusion, deduction, or recommendation—often an opinion or theory to articulate an argument—the topic is more accurately called a *claim*, like: *Red delicious apples taste best*. In fact, for such instances I recommend using the word *claim* in lieu of *topic* on the Evidence Finder.

Quote (Evidence): I recommend completing the quote box next. Even though a context box is placed before the quote box in the Evidence Finder (and it's in that order for a reason), field testing has shown that identifying the quotation before establishing context is easier for students. Most of the time, a 1–2 sentence quotation is sufficient for a piece of evidence. Occasionally a longer quotation is needed, and the box is too small. In such instances, have students write on the back, or teach them to use an ellipsis to omit superfluous information. A word of caution: an ellipsis may allow time to retrieve the entire quote later, but students can absentmindedly leave out the rest of the quote when they transfer their data from the Evidence Finder to a paragraph. For this reason, when possible, I try to encourage writing the entire quote (legibly) for later use. For teachers who employ MLA citation, you can add parentheses at the end of your quote boxes for page numbers.

For clarification, sometimes students think that in order to capture a piece of evidence from a text that the quotation has to have quotation marks around it already (because, after all, they are being asked to put quotation marks around the evidence they are finding). Obviously this is not the case. A student may gather either a narrative or literary (also called dialogic) quotation. I term a narrative quotation as one where the narrator (or author) has written something inside the paragraph worthy of quoting; I term a literary (or dialogic) quote as one where a character talks to another inside the story (like Gepetto to Pinocchio) or article (like a journalist interviewing someone). Interestingly, I have not always found it necessary to teach this distinction to my students. When they find out they can use any portion of a text, whether it initially has quotation marks or not, such awareness seems sufficient.

Context: Context is the information surrounding the text (see the Critical Thinking Map). Context may be *narrative* (context of the author); or *literary* (context of the character), also called *dialogic*. And sometimes students mix the two. Examples from *Pinocchio* provide a figure below:

Figure 3.2 Establishing Context

Narrative (context of the author)		Literary (context of the character)		Mixed	
WHO	**TO WHOM**	**WHO**	**TO WHOM**	**WHO**	**TO WHOM**
Author Carlo Collodi	Young children	Gepetto	Pinocchio	Author Carlo Collodi	Young Children
WHEN	**WHERE**	**WHEN**	**WHERE**	**WHEN**	**WHERE**
1883	The Adventures of Pinocchio	On the first evening	Inside his workshop	On the first evening	Inside his workshop

I find that most students navigate the context portion of the Evidence Finder fairly well, especially with guidance. They are keen to observe instances where the fine print of an article may reveal, for example, additional context clues they can cram into their boxes. They also enjoy sounding a little "fancy" by adding relevant details. For example, instead of writing "reader" or "audience" in the "to whom" box, they enjoy (and you might encourage) writing "young readers" or even better "young readers who enjoy sports." Narrowing the audience or speculating on the perceived audience will help students target the author's possible intentions, a point that will later enhance their elaboration. Discernment as to what to include or exclude in these boxes comes with practice. If there is to be a problem, mixing contexts on the Evidence Finder could be one culprit for trouble when writing a paragraph later. It depends on how students lead into their quotation. A student might write:

Figure 3.3 Establishing Context—Student Sample

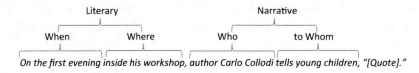

On the first evening inside his workshop, author Carlo Collodi tells young children, "[Quote]."

Written this way makes it sound as though the author was inside the workshop talking, when it was actually Gepetto talking. Redirection from a teacher should help the student correct the confusion:

Collodi tells young children that on the first evening inside the woodcarver's workshop, the puppet maker Gepetto talks to his new creation, saying, "[Quote]."

Just be mindful of the narrative-literary distinction, even if you choose not to teach it. It may help you trouble-shoot when co-writing subsequent paragraphs with your students. And a quick reminder: when an author's name is captured in an introductory paragraph, a writer will need to be cautious about over-using it when providing a contextual attribution. Teach students how to use synonyms. If Abraham Lincoln is quoted, for example, then students might use alternatives in subsequent references: Lincoln (last name only), the president, the statesman, the Civil War leader, the commander-in-chief, etc. When the author is anonymous, remind students of additional options beyond the word *author*: writer, narrator, storyteller, researcher, dramatist, essayist, journalist, poet, editor, scribe, etc.

Explain the Quote: In this box students rewrite the quote in their own words in roughly the same length as the quotation. You may prefer the word *paraphrase* instead of the expression "explain the quote." I use the latter because it seems to be easier for students to remember. I gradually introduce the word *paraphrase* once "explain the quote" (as part of The Secret Recipe) has been repeated enough to solidify memory. For young writers, I would recommend teaching them to use the word "here" as a crutch word or key word to begin their explanations: **Here** *Gepetto gives his new creation a name, like he would a real boy.* Or: **Here** *the researcher explains how obesity affects respiratory function.* After students get the hang of paraphrasing, the key word "here" naturally drops off and only reappears when preference dictates.

Analyze (Elaborate, Reason, Rationalize, or Explore): The concept of *analysis* seems to be used in two ways: first as a catch-all word used by the public to describe critical thinking generally; and second in a deconstructive sense, as an academic might disassemble something into its parts and relationships. Put another way, general use of the word seems to include all 12 Tools, but academic (and more accurate) use includes essentially only Tools #5 and #6, Make a List and Find a Link, respectively.

Analysis on the Evidence Finder is (for better or worse) meant to capture all critical thinking. If my word choice does not suit your situation, it's an easy change: for states or countries that use different nomenclature, substitute the word that most closely aligns with *elaboration, reasoning,* or *exploration*. Whatever the term, this is the portion where we want students to engage the evidence they have provided to offer interpretations, find insights, or make assertions that reflect upon or engage their evidence. This is where I would teach students to "stack" their responses, jumping from one tool to another as they elaborate further (assuming, of course, that their responses relate to their claim). Do not underestimate the word "if" to create the conditional and "because" to allow evidence or logic.

For instances when The 12 Tools have not been taught, a few **key words** can help students at least complete this box of in the Evidence Finder with a sentence or two:

This shows (proves)...	If..., then...	Clearly,...	likely, probably
This suggests...	should, would, could	Evidently,...	because
It seems...	might, must, will	As a result,...	
It appears...	The evidence illustrates...	The effect will be...	

Evidence Finder Options

Evidence Finders on the next few pages vary in the number of evidences you want students to find, 1.0–4.0. A one-piece finder is a good starting point, and it features blank lines at the bottom on which students can then use The Secret Recipe to write a paragraph. Using a two-piece finder lends itself to a multi-quote or a multi-source paragraphs, and blank lines also fit at the bottom. Using a three-piece or four-piece finder might also allow for students to write a multi-paragraph essay.

Figure 3.4 Evidence Finder 1.0

EVIDENCE FINDER 1.0   Name: _____

What do you want to find?

I want to find evidence of _____.

1 TOPIC Example or Claim	CONTEXT		QUOTE	EXPLAIN THE QUOTE	ANALYSIS Elaboration or Rationale
	WHO	TO WHOM			
	WHEN	WHERE			

Figure 3.5 Evidence Finder 2.0

EVIDENCE FINDER 2.0   Name: _____

I want to find evidence of _____ .

1 TOPIC Example or Claim	CONTEXT		QUOTE	EXPLAIN THE QUOTE	ANALYSIS Elaboration or Rationale
	WHO	TO WHOM			
	WHEN	WHERE			

2 TOPIC Example or Claim	CONTEXT		QUOTE	EXPLAIN THE QUOTE	ANALYSIS Elaboration or Rationale
	WHO	TO WHOM			
	WHEN	WHERE			

_____
_____
_____
_____
_____
_____
_____

Figure 3.6 Evidence Finder 2.1 (Text to Self)

EVIDENCE FINDER 2.1 (Text to Self)   Name: _____

I want to find evidence of (how) _____ (relates to my own life).

From the text

1 TOPIC EXAMPLE or CLAIM	CONTEXT		QUOTE	EXPLAIN THE QUOTE	ANALYSIS ELABORATE
	WHO	TO WHOM			
	WHEN	WHERE			

From my own life

2 TOPIC EVENT	CONTEXT		PERSONAL EXPERIENCE		CONNECTION
	WHO WAS THERE				
	WHEN	WHERE			

_____
_____
_____
_____
_____
_____
_____

Figure 3.7 Evidence Finder 3.0

EVIDENCE FINDER 3.0   Name: _____

I want to find evidence of _____.

1	TOPIC	CONTEXT		QUOTE	EXPLAIN THE QUOTE	ANALYSIS
	Example or Claim	WHO	TO WHOM			Elaboration
		WHEN	WHERE			

2	TOPIC	CONTEXT		QUOTE	EXPLAIN THE QUOTE	ANALYSIS
	Example or Claim	WHO	TO WHOM			Elaboration
		WHEN	WHERE			

3	TOPIC	CONTEXT		QUOTE	EXPLAIN THE QUOTE	ANALYSIS
	Example or Claim	WHO	TO WHOM			Elaboration
		WHEN	WHERE			

Figure 3.8 Evidence Finder 4.0

EVIDENCE FINDER 4.0   Name: _____

I want to find evidence of _____.

1	TOPIC	CONTEXT		QUOTE	EXPLAIN THE QUOTE	ANALYSIS
	EXAMPLE or CLAIM	WHO	TO WHOM			Elaboration
		WHEN	WHERE			

2	TOPIC	CONTEXT		QUOTE	EXPLAIN THE QUOTE	ANALYSIS
	EXAMPLE or CLAIM	WHO	TO WHOM			Elaboration
		WHEN	WHERE			

3	TOPIC	CONTEXT		QUOTE	EXPLAIN THE QUOTE	ANALYSIS
	EXAMPLE or CLAIM	WHO	TO WHOM			Elaboration
		WHEN	WHERE			

4	TOPIC	CONTEXT		QUOTE	EXPLAIN THE QUOTE	ANALYSIS
	EXAMPLE or CLAIM	WHO	TO WHOM			Elaboration
		WHEN	WHERE			

The size and scope of your question will naturally lend itself to the Evidence Finder you choose. For example, if you want to compare two stories, students will need (at a minimum) a two-row finder, so that they can procure one piece of evidence from both stories. If you want students to compare *and* contrast two stories, students will need (at a minimum) four evidence rows, one piece of evidence from each story to show similarity and one piece of evidence from each story to show difference.

4

The Secret Recipe

Many years ago I sat down with a young man in a one-on-one writing conference to examine his essay. As was common, this young man's paper lacked cohesion and substance. I remember him wanting to do well, but clearly he was lost writing a paragraph, especially one with evidence. Probably in a tone that must have revealed my frustration, I said, "Alright, look: Let me write an example for you on the board." I took his claim and evidence and slowly wrote a paragraph on the board behind us. I then labeled the parts—or functions—of the paragraph. I turned around and asked, "Do you understand now?" His response was truthfully unexpected:

"Yeah, I get it."

What? Really? I looked up. (We had been working at this awhile.) We both stared at the board, and after a long pause I concurred: "Yeah, me too." It was very humbling to discover that the reason so many of my students' papers were lacking was because of my poor teaching. I hadn't explained the process well. Even with all of those conferences, the paragraph's functions were in essence camouflaged for me until that moment. I must have only intuitively understood the process through my own writing experience. It seems in college we are expected to write well, but this is very different from teaching writing. I stopped the class and reiterated the example on the board. They, too, agreed that the process was easier to understand and immediately students' papers jumped in quality.

On that day The Secret Recipe was born. Please forgive two things: first, the moniker "The Secret Recipe." I needed a name on the spur of the moment that would spark my students' curiosity. It worked, so I have been using it ever since. And second, forgive my calling it a *secret*; the functions are well-known. Years of teaching have taught me that others have equally valuable methods for designing evidence-based paragraphs. The Secret Recipe is my favorite because the framework is so simple (perhaps deceptively simple), like the folds of a paper clip that takes an ordinary piece of wire and with exactly the right bends creates a valuable tool.

As I have suggested, The Secret Recipe is only one structure for writing an evidence-based paragraph, and it is not meant for an introduction or conclusion of an essay. It has proven effective as a **short-answer response** (like on a test or as a verbal response in class) or as a **supporting paragraph** in the body of a paper. It aligns exactly with the Evidence Finder, moving left to right. When students get started, normally one piece of evidence (or evidence row) creates one paragraph:

The Secret Recipe

1. **TOPIC**
   (Example or Claim)

2. **CONTEXT**

3. **QUOTE**
   (Evidence)

4. **EXPLAIN THE QUOTE**

5. **ANALYSIS**
   (Elaboration)

Some experts caution teachers regarding the use of writing structures; after all, we do not want students' writing to sound formulaic, which is to remove students' originality or creativity. I use the analogy of making cookies to illustrate what I advocate for students in this regard: when making cookies, we follow a certain recipe to obtain a desired result. What happens if we don't follow the recipe?—if we take our flour, eggs, sugar, and chocolate chips and place them in a bowl or cold oven? Are we going to produce good-tasting cookies? Certainly not. Then I go on to explain that many of their moms have been making cookies for a long time, and they have learned how to make certain changes (like mixing or replacing ingredients) without compromising the desired result: a delicious cookie.

Writing with evidence may be understood in the same way: once students understand the basic functions and can use the recipe correctly, their natural inclination is to explore further—without compromising the functions or paragraph.

Just a few words on each function:

1. **Topic (or Claim):** A topic sentence or claim is usually the teacher's question restated plus the reason or example students have identified in the text, all in one solid sentence. (The 12 Tools can help create these.) Once students get the hang of it, they learn that they can add other sentences that define or elaborate on the topic.

   Baseline length: 1 sentence
   Advanced length: 2–3 sentences

2. **Context:** A common source of consternation for teachers is when students summarize a text when they have been asked to respond to a text. By asking students to provide the context—*who, to whom, when, and where*—as a means to lead into a quotation, it places a sensible parameter around such information until they learn that the context can be expanded, as long as it doesn't prove superfluous.

   Baseline length: 1 subordinate clause—1 sentence
   Advanced length: 2–3 sentences

3. **Quote (Evidence):** Evidence can come in multiple forms, but I have found that a quotation from a text is actually the most concrete and therefore a good starting point for students. More abstract forms of evidence may include paraphrased information, in which case the "Explain the quote" portion is no longer needed; and anecdotal or observational evidence, perhaps from their own lives (See Evidence Finder 2.1 [Text to Self]). When students gather evidence from a nonfiction source, you will likely have an opportunity to differentiate between fact and opinion. Facts are usually better, but remember that facts can be overly generalized or off-topic, and seemingly lesser-important opinions may actually be stronger if the person quoted is credentialed. This is also a good time to teach the difference between primary and secondary sources.

   Baseline length: 1 phrase/clause—2 sentences
   Advanced length: As needed

4. **Explain the Quote:** Not every quote needs an explanation, like when a quotation is self-evident; however, I try to encourage an explanation in most cases. It's good for students to practice, and for me to check for understanding. Obviously, explanations (or paraphrasing) are particularly helpful when a quotation

uses complex wording. I have found that the ordinary task of paraphrasing is more difficult than it should be (and may be the result of poor reading practice).

Baseline length: 1 sentence
Advanced length: As needed

5. **Analyze (Elaborate):** To complete a baseline paragraph, students need only add one or more reflective sentences at the end, which is to demonstrate how their piece of evidence justifies their claim. Again, this word *analysis* (in the general sense) may be substituted for *elaboration, rationale, exploration, expansion, reflection, reasoning, justification*, or some other word preferred in your state or district. **Key words** mentioned in Chapter 3 can help. Applicable tools in The 12 Tools will enhance the paragraph beyond the baseline.

Baseline length: 1–2 sentences
Advanced length: As needed

An Example

The following example will illustrate The Secret Recipe. For this assignment students read William Shakespeare's *Romeo and Juliet* and then determine whether it was Juliet's or Romeo's fault for the relationship failing. Provided with two copies of Evidence Finder 3.0, one for Romeo and one for Juliet, students find evidence for both sides but choose one side on which to write an essay. A young student might complete an Evidence Finder in this manner:

I want to find evidence of *Juliet's mistakes that caused her relationship with Romeo to fail.*

Figure 4.1 Evidence Finder—*Romeo and Juliet*

1 TOPIC	CONTEXT		QUOTE	EXPLAIN THE QUOTE	ANALYSIS
Declares love too early	**WHO** Juliet	**TO WHOM** To herself	"Romeo, Romeo! Wherefore art thou Romeo? Deny thy father and refuse thy name! Or, if thou wilt not, be but sworn my love, and I'll no longer be a Capulet" (1023).	Juliet calls for Romeo and wants him to forsake his name, but if he cannot, she will give up her last name of Capulet to be with him.	Juliet should have kept her feelings to herself. She needed time to figure out what to do next.
	WHEN After the Capulet party	**WHERE** On the balcony			

After writing an introduction that included mentioning the play, author, and thesis, she uses her completed Evidence Finder to write a baseline supporting paragraph using The Secret Recipe. (Key words have been underlined for illustration.) Our attention is on the supporting paragraph (with each function labeled for easier reference):

Figure 4.2 Baseline Paragraph (Single Quote)—*Romeo and Juliet*

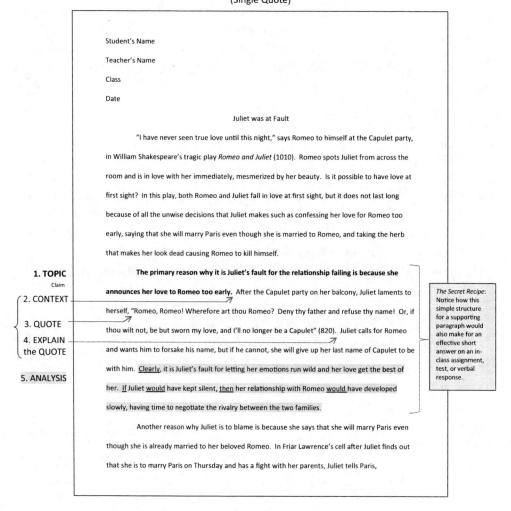

The Secret Recipe may also be utilized for a **multi-quote** or **multi-source** paragraph by simply repeating the evidence core (numbers 2–4):

Figure 4.3 Multi-Quote/Multi-Source Paragraph—*Romeo and Juliet*

Multi-quote/Multi-source

1. Topic (or Claim)
   - 2. Context
   - 3. Quote
   - 4. Explain the Quote
   - 2. Context
   - 3. Quote
   - 4. Explain the Quote
5. Analysis (or Elaboration)

Students may opt to analyze after each explanation or all at the end, depending on what's best for the situation.

What if a student wanted to blame both Romeo *and* Juliet for their relationship failing? This would be a great opportunity to write a multi-quote response. (Compare-contrast paragraphs also work really well using this two-part structure.) A supporting paragraph might read:

Figure 4.4 Baseline Paragraph (Multi-Quote)—*Romeo and Juliet*

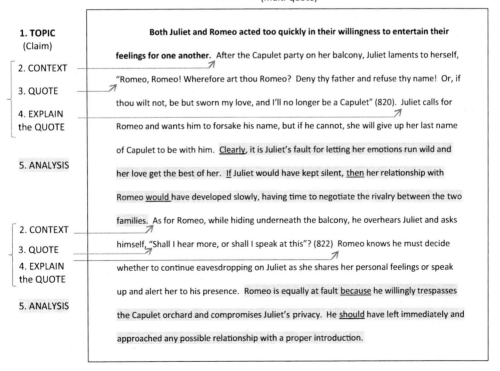

BASELINE PARAGRAPH
(multi-quote)

1. TOPIC (Claim)
2. CONTEXT
3. QUOTE
4. EXPLAIN the QUOTE
5. ANALYSIS

2. CONTEXT
3. QUOTE
4. EXPLAIN the QUOTE
5. ANALYSIS

Both Juliet and Romeo acted too quickly in their willingness to entertain their feelings for one another. After the Capulet party on her balcony, Juliet laments to herself, "Romeo, Romeo! Wherefore art thou Romeo? Deny thy father and refuse thy name! Or, if thou wilt not, be but sworn my love, and I'll no longer be a Capulet" (820). Juliet calls for Romeo and wants him to forsake his name, but if he cannot, she will give up her last name of Capulet to be with him. Clearly, it is Juliet's fault for letting her emotions run wild and her love get the best of her. If Juliet would have kept silent, then her relationship with Romeo would have developed slowly, having time to negotiate the rivalry between the two families. As for Romeo, while hiding underneath the balcony, he overhears Juliet and asks himself, "Shall I hear more, or shall I speak at this"? (822) Romeo knows he must decide whether to continue eavesdropping on Juliet as she shares her personal feelings or speak up and alert her to his presence. Romeo is equally at fault because he willingly trespasses the Capulet orchard and compromises Juliet's privacy. He should have left immediately and approached any possible relationship with a proper introduction.

Optional Scaffolding

If you teach younger students, or if you teach those who need extra help, you may consider providing them with a template, Figure 4.5 or Figure 4.6, for The Secret Recipe as well. With each piece given its own line, a teacher can easily determine which, if any, steps are causing the student to struggle in their transfer of information from the Evidence Finder to a baseline paragraph.

Also, students can use the same structure to help them frame their verbal responses. I recommend encouraging their practice. For this purpose, I have die-cut steps to The Secret Recipe permanently posted on my walls, as well as for easy reference during one-on-one conferences.

Remember The 12 Tools *can* help students write their claims *and* enhance their elaboration. This author shares the point of view that one paragraph written well is worth considerably more than an entire essay written poorly. Also, you will note that sometimes No. 5, *Analysis* (or *Elaboration*) can take place after each No. 4, *Explain the Quote*, respectively, or, all at the end of the paragraph, whichever is better for the situation.

Figure 4.5 Secret Recipe for Single Quote Paragraph

Supporting Paragraph
(Single Quote)

Topic (or Claim): _____

Context: _____

Quote: _____

Explain the Quote: _____

Analysis (Or Elaboration): _____

Figure 4.6 Secret Recipe for Multi-Quote Paragraph

Supporting Paragraph
(Multi-quote)

1. Topic (or Claim): _____

2. Context: _____
3. Quote: _____
4. Explain the Quote: _____

2. Context: _____
3. Quote: _____
4. Explain the Quote: _____

Analysis (Or Elaboration): _____

5

Guided Practice

You have now been introduced to the following:

1. A Critical Thinking Map to guide you as you create varied combinations of reader-response questions or prompts for your students;
2. The 12 Tools to simplify critical thinking;
3. An Evidence Finder to aid in gathering, organizing, and responding to evidence; and
4. The Secret Recipe to guide an evidence-based paragraph (which will then be enhanced using The 12 Tools).

You are now ready to see all four tools used together.

Baseline Examples

Because these are the first full-process models you will see, the steps are demonstrated more slowly and with greater detail.

The first two—*Cinderella* and *Goldilocks and the Three Bears*—are meant to serve as a starting point because most readers are familiar with them. The next three examples—*Hatchet* by Gary Paulsen, *The Giver* by Lois Lowry, and the *Gettysburg Address* by President Abraham Lincoln—will provide more realistic in-class examples with the same step-by-step attention.

Guided Practice: *Cinderella*

TEXT AND GOAL: Ms. Clark wants her students to practice a character analysis using a text with which they are already familiar—*Cinderella*. In this way she can teach the process first. Through reading, media, and class discussion, most students know the story and can explain the characters' relationships. Ms. Clark now wants her students to move beyond knowledge and comprehension into deeper-level skill sets. Specifically, she wants to ask a text-dependent question that will require students to gather evidence from the text, organize it (into an Evidence Finder), write a solid response (using The Secret Recipe), and deepen that response (using their Critical Thinking Tools). She determines a character analysis would be a good starting point and is ready to design a question.

Using the Map

Step 1: To study Cinderella's character, Ms. Clark knows she must have her students examine the text, specifically the *Ideas and Content* of the text.

Step 2: She decides that she will have students place a value (*Evaluation*) on the character Cinderella in some way.

Step 3: To design a question, she chooses Tool #3 *"Agree or Disagree?"* to allow them to decide their position based on their understanding.

She knows when students use the word "because" to explain their rationales, they will naturally shift from *comprehension* (understanding the story like they already do) to *construction* (which will require them to make a claim) and *evaluation* (weighing something in Cinderella's demeanor or actions). She has a combination or pathway.

CREATING THE QUESTION: In a few moments, Ms. Clark has brainstormed a few options:

- Do you agree or disagree with Cinderella's decision to leave the ball?
- Do you agree or disagree with Cinderella hiding her identity from the Prince?
- Do you agree or disagree with the idea that Cinderella is a confident person? OR: Is Cinderella a confident person?

While all good options, she decides the last one may expand students' search throughout the whole story, potentially giving them greater opportunity to find inferences to support their opinion.

FINDING EVIDENCE: To guide their practice, Ms. Clark passes out a copy of the story and an Evidence Finder to each student and then projects the finder onto her white board. In this way, she can demonstrate the process of preparing one's evidence by filling out the organizer with them. She asks the question (or writes off to the side): *Is Cinderella a confident person? Support your answer.*

They read the story. Ms. Clark invites students to pinpoint the textual evidence by raising their hands when they find a possibility, or by marking or highlighting the passage in some way. Each example helps her create a list of instances where Cinderella was confident and unconfident:

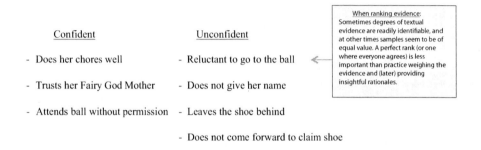

After some discussion, students decide that they "agree" *and* "disagree" with the idea that Cinderella is confident—but mostly disagree. They finally decide and the teacher writes the focus in the blank provided. Students do the same. She uses five separate colors to improve distinction and clarity.

Figure 5.1 Evidence Finder Template

I want to find evidence of **how Cinderella is unconfident**.

TOPIC	CONTEXT		QUOTE	EXPLAIN THE QUOTE	ANALYSIS
	WHO	TO WHOM			
	WHEN	WHERE			

Ms. Clark helps students prioritize their evidence, from strongest to weakest. She explains that the **topic** is likely the example that demonstrates whether or not Cinderella is confident. Together they determine Cinderella's decision to withhold her name when they were dancing is the best example of her lacking confidence.

Figure 5.2 Evidence Finder: Choosing a Topic

TOPIC	CONTEXT		QUOTE	EXPLAIN THE QUOTE	ANALYSIS
Does not give her name	WHO	TO WHOM	"The monarch clearly favored the waltz, and upon bowing, renewed the spectacle each dance as he accompanied Cinderella to his lavish ballroom Floor."		
	WHEN	WHERE			

Next, a student reads the **evidence** previously discovered, while Ms. Clark writes the quotation in the space provided. Students do the same in their Evidence Finders. (This quote, by the way, was created by the author for demonstration purposes only.)

Once the evidence has been recorded, have students write the context next. Ms. Clark asks, "Who said this?" pointing to the quote, followed by, "To whom was the author speaking?" She writes their answers.

Figure 5.3 Evidence Finder: Identifying Context

TOPIC	CONTEXT		QUOTE	EXPLAIN THE QUOTE	ANALYSIS
Does not give her name	WHO Author	TO WHOM Reader	"The monarch clearly favored the waltz, and upon bowing, renewed the spectacle each dance as he accompanied the beautiful stranger to his lavish ballroom floor."		
	WHEN After arriving at the ball	WHERE At the Prince's castle			

Ms. Clark continues: "When did the author say this?" Here's the tricky part: Is the teacher asking, "What year did the author write this?" or "When did this quote take place in the story?" Obviously the latter suits our needs in this instance. Sometimes students may need to record a time, day, month, or year, but it is as equally helpful to use time-indicative words like *before*, *after*, *during*, *upon*, *when*, or *while* to write a small clause or phrase in the box. Students decide on "After arriving at the ball"—and for *where*: "At the Prince's castle."

Explain the Quote: One way to check for understanding is to have students paraphrase or explain the evidence in their own words. Sometimes quotations are self-explanatory; others need clarification. Either way, students need the practice. (See also Figure 5.38 on page 103.)

Ms. Clark continues by explaining that one "trick" to explaining a quotation is to begin with the word "Here," followed by the person talking, in this case "narrator" because the class already used "author" in the context. Next she needs a strong verb that matches what the author is doing.

Ms. Clark writes on her evidence finder: "Here the narrator—" and then interrupts, "What is the narrator doing? The narrator *states?—explains?—describes?—relates?—depicts?—posits?*" Students verbally choose "describes" and she adds it to the evidence finder. "Now help me," she solicits further, "complete the sentence." With a little help, students finish the explanation.

Figure 5.4 Evidence Finder: Explaining the Quote

TOPIC	CONTEXT		QUOTE	EXPLAIN THE QUOTE	ANALYSIS
Does not give her name	WHO Author	TO WHOM Reader	"The monarch clearly favored the waltz, and upon bowing, renewed the spectacle each dance as he accompanied the beautiful stranger to his lavish ballroom floor."	Here the narrator describes how the Prince asks Cinderella to dance multiple times but does not know her name.	
	WHEN After arriving at the ball	WHERE At the Prince's castle			

As this is their first time drawing a conclusion, Ms. Clark writes "This shows" in the Analysis (or Elaboration) box of the Evidence Finder and then asks: "What have we shown?" If students pause, she points to the top line of the Evidence Finder and follows with "For what purpose have we been finding evidence? To show . . .?" Inevitably, students respond with "that Cinderella is unconfident." Ms. Clark continues writing, "This shows that Cinderella is unconfident (brainstorming the synonym *insecure*) because . . . ," and students help complete the line.

Figure 5.5 Evidence Finder: Drawing a Conclusion

I want to find evidence of **how Cinderella is unconfident.**

TOPIC	CONTEXT		QUOTE	EXPLAIN THE QUOTE	ANALYSIS
Does not give her name	**WHO** Author	**TO WHOM** Reader	"The monarch clearly favored the waltz, and upon bowing, renewed the spectacle each dance as he accompanied the beautiful stranger to his lavish ballroom floor."	Here the narrator describes how the Prince asks Cinderella to dance multiple times but does not know her name.	This shows that Cinderella is insecure because she deliberately avoids several chances to give her name while dancing with the Prince.
	WHEN After arriving at the ball	**WHERE** At the Prince's castle			

THE SECRET RECIPE

Once the Evidence Finder is complete, students are now ready to write a single, albeit very basic, evidence-based paragraph. Ms. Clark uses another board to co-write a paragraph with students. She writes the functions of The Secret Recipe along the left side of the board and leaves room on the right to draft a sample. To write the topic sentence, Ms. Clark helps them see that by restating the teacher's question (essentially the "I want to find evidence of" line at the top) and the topic—both in blue in the digital version—students construct a workable topic sentence:

1. **Topic** (or **Claim**) ⟶ Cinderella is an unconfident person because she withheld her name from the Prince.
2. Context
3. "Quote"
4. Explain the Quote
5. Analysis

Writing the context takes a little practice, and if there is a spot where students may mess up, it's here. Ms. Clark explains that students may write the "who, to whom, when, and where" in any order to introduce the quote—as long as it makes sense. (This particular example will be a little more difficult because it mixes literary—*when* and *where* inside the story—and narrative—*who* and *to whom* outside the story—contexts.) A student offers an attempt:

After arriving at the ball at the Prince's castle, the author says to the reader,

The challenge becomes evident: this attempt makes it sound as if the author is attending the ball. Ms. Clark explains that students (1) can use whatever wording is necessary to make the context boxes clear, including multiple sentences; and (2) not every part of the context needs to be used. Finally students are able to work through this and arrive at the following:

After Cinderella arrives at the Prince's castle, she goes inside to attend the ball. The author relates,

In this example, students choose to omit the "to whom" portion of the context. The remaining portion of the paragraph comes verbatim from the Evidence Finder, though obviously students are at liberty to change the wording at any time. Ms. Clark uses the same colors to help students differentiate the functions as they have learned them in The Secret Recipe:

Figure 5.6 *Cinderella* Paragraph—Baseline Version

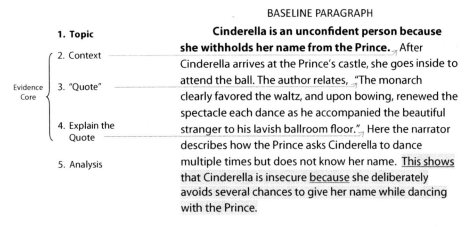

Critical Thinking

Ms. Clark now wants students to add depth to their baseline paragraph. She asks students to take out their 12 Critical Thinking Tools reference sheets (with Sentence Starters), while she takes out her teacher version (with Question Starters). She reminds students that they can now jump around from tool to tool, as long as it relates to Cinderella's lack of confidence.

She notices a few tools easily relate to their conversation and uses them to help students:

Figure 5.7 Tool #6: Find a Link

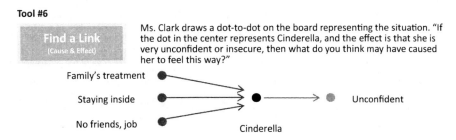

Students posit that her family's negative treatment likely caused much of Cinderella's shyness. They believe staying inside for chores all the time prohibited her opportunities to gain experience or find successes outside the home, professionally or socially.

Figure 5.8 Tool #7: If ..., then ...

Tool #7

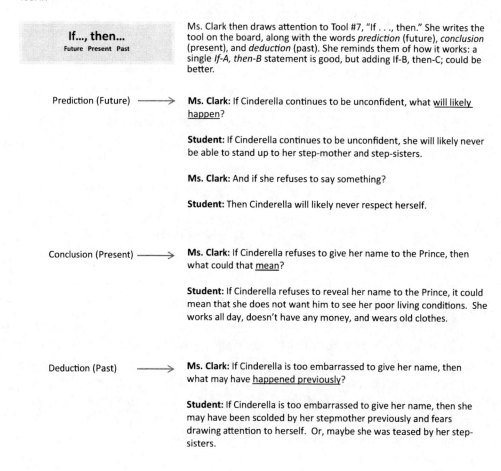

Ms. Clark then draws attention to Tool #7, "If . . ., then." She writes the tool on the board, along with the words *prediction* (future), *conclusion* (present), and *deduction* (past). She reminds them of how it works: a single *If-A, then-B* statement is good, but adding If-B, then-C; could be better.

Prediction (Future) →

Ms. Clark: If Cinderella continues to be unconfident, what <u>will likely happen</u>?

Student: If Cinderella continues to be unconfident, she will likely never be able to stand up to her step-mother and step-sisters.

Ms. Clark: And if she refuses to say something?

Student: Then Cinderella will likely never respect herself.

Conclusion (Present) →

Ms. Clark: If Cinderella refuses to give her name to the Prince, then what could that <u>mean</u>?

Student: If Cinderella refuses to reveal her name to the Prince, it could mean that she does not want him to see her poor living conditions. She works all day, doesn't have any money, and wears old clothes.

Deduction (Past) →

Ms. Clark: If Cinderella is too embarrassed to give her name, then what may have <u>happened previously</u>?

Student: If Cinderella is too embarrassed to give her name, then she may have been scolded by her stepmother previously and fears drawing attention to herself. Or, maybe she was teased by her step-sisters.

Tool #8

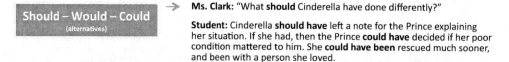

Ms. Clark: "What **should** Cinderella have done differently?"

Student: Cinderella **should have** left a note for the Prince explaining her situation. If she had, then the Prince **could have** decided if her poor condition mattered to him. She **could have been** rescued much sooner, and been with a person she loved.

Now with a series of analytic insights, Ms. Clark's class is able to enhance the quality of their paragraph. The new version looks something like this:

Figure 5.9 *Cinderella* Paragraph - New Version

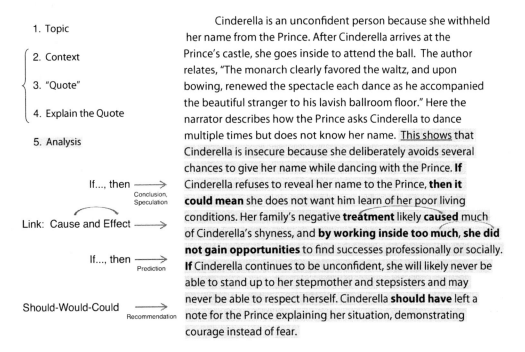

By "stacking" their analysis—using multiple tools in succession—Ms. Clark's class is able to write a solid evidentiary-based paragraph with deeper critical thinking. One nuanced reminder for teachers to give students: the word "then" in an "If-then" statement may be omitted; we know even the word "if" may be rephrased and still convey a conditional. Tools naturally overlap. A "Should-would-could" statement may easily merge with an "If-then" statement or a "Cause and Effect" statement. Students' disjunctive comments at first become more cohesive with practice.

Guided Practice: *Goldilocks and the Three Bears*

TEXT AND GOAL: Mr. Gatewood wants his students to write a critical response to text. To learn the process, he decides to use *Goldilocks and the*

Three Bears as a baseline to teach the process of finding evidence (Evidence Finder), writing an evidentiary-based paragraph (The Secret Recipe), and enhancing critical thinking (The 12 Tools). He wants students to use *multiple texts*, one fiction and one nonfiction source. He has an idea of what he wants his question to be, but he wants to verify that his assignment will touch on a variety of cognitive levels. His idea: He wants to see if Goldilocks would be convicted as a felon according to local laws. (The author created the quote for demonstration.)

Using the Map

Step 1: Mr. Gatewood chooses to examine the text, specifically the *Ideas and Content* of both texts.

Step 2: He decides on two pathways: First students will analyze *(Analysis)* both texts, searching for connections between the story and statute. He also wants students to form a claim (that is, *to Create*) an opinion and then integrate evidence from both texts.

Step 3: To design a question, he chooses *Tool #8 "Should, Would, Could"* to allow them to decide their position based on what they find in the criminal code.

CREATING THE QUESTION: Mr. Gatewood knows students' practice analyzing the literature will come from making a list of possible crimes in the story and matching them with possible misdemeanors or felonies they find in the statute. However, beyond the analytic or deconstructive exercise of making lists and connections, Mr. Gatewood wants his students to form a hypothesis (in other words, make a claim) and offer evidence and rationale to defend their position. He decides on the following:

- In the fairy tale *Goldilocks and the Three Bears*, according to the criminal code, *should* Goldilocks be convicted of a crime?

FINDING EVIDENCE: Mr. Gatewood draws his students' attention atop the *Evidence Finder*, guiding them to complete the sentence:

I want to find evidence of *Goldilocks' possible unlawful conduct according to the criminal code.*

After reading the story, Mr. Gatewood asks students to identify possible crimes that Goldilocks committed and list them on the board. Next he has them read the criminal code of their state's statutes. A simple Compare T-chart (two *lists* aligned) helps them make the necessary connections:

Figure 5.10 Compare T-Chart—*Goldilocks and the Three Bears*

Goldilocks	Criminal Code		Bonus: Connection Type
* Enters Bears' home	* Criminal trespassing	→	behavioral, legal
* Eats their food	* Criminal burglary	→	behavioral, legal
* Breaks kitchen chair	* Criminal damage	→	behavioral, legal

Mr. Gatewood realizes that he will need three pairs of Evidence Finder rows, one for each connection. In process, Mr. Gatewood discovers two people technically speak in the first piece of evidence—Goldilocks who asks the question and the narrator who continues to tell the story; second, the contextual "when" of the criminal code does not seem particularly relevant; and third, that he and his students cannot draw any conclusions till they have both pieces of evidence, hence the empty space:

Figure 5.11 Evidence Finder—*Goldilocks and the Three Bears*

Goldilocks

1 TOPIC	CONTEXT		QUOTE	EXPLAIN THE QUOTE	ANALYSIS
Enters Bears' Home	WHO Goldilocks & the narrator	TO WHOM Possibly bears & readers	"'Anyone home?' she called, gazing round the door. Then she went into the empty house and started to explore the kitchen."	Goldilocks enters the Bears' home without permission, knowing they were not home.	
Criminal Code	WHEN After knocking	WHERE The Bears' home			

2 TOPIC	CONTEXT		QUOTE	EXPLAIN THE QUOTE	ANALYSIS
Criminal Tres-passing	WHO State statute	TO WHOM Citizens	"A person commits criminal trespass in the first degree by knowingly: 1. Entering or remaining unlawfully in or on a residential structure… a class 1 misdemeanor"	Criminal trespassing requires knowingly entering a residence without permission.	Goldilocks breaks the law because she knows no one is home and enters anyway, a misdemeanor in the criminal code.
	WHEN (not applicable)	WHERE Criminal Code 13-1504			

84 ◆ Guided Practice

The process is repeated for the final two connections. Mr. Gatewood facilitates the first paragraph:

Figure 5.12 *Goldilocks and the Three Bears* Paragraph—Baseline Version

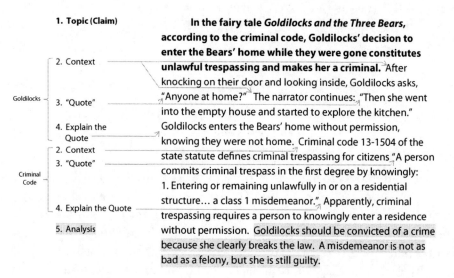

Mr. Gatewood is pleased with their baseline paragraph but wants students to analyze the situation further. He uses the critical thinking tools (the initial question projected onto the board) to help students deepen their reasoning:

Figure 5.13 Critical Thinking Tools

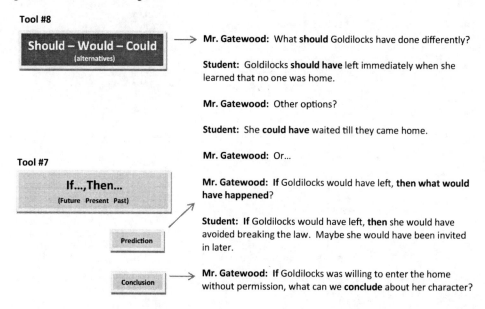

Figure 5.13 Continued

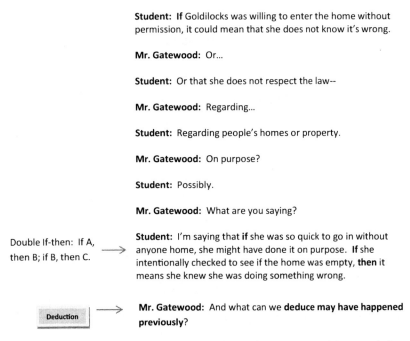

Student: If Goldilocks was willing to enter the home without permission, it could mean that she does not know it's wrong.

Mr. Gatewood: Or...

Student: Or that she does not respect the law--

Mr. Gatewood: Regarding...

Student: Regarding people's homes or property.

Mr. Gatewood: On purpose?

Student: Possibly.

Mr. Gatewood: What are you saying?

Student: I'm saying that **if** she was so quick to go in without anyone home, she might have done it on purpose. **If** she intentionally checked to see if the home was empty, **then** it means she knew she was doing something wrong.

Mr. Gatewood: And what can we **deduce may have happened previously**?

Student: It's possible that she has committed this crime before.

Figure 5.14 *Goldilocks and the Three Bears* Paragraph - New Version

NEW VERSION

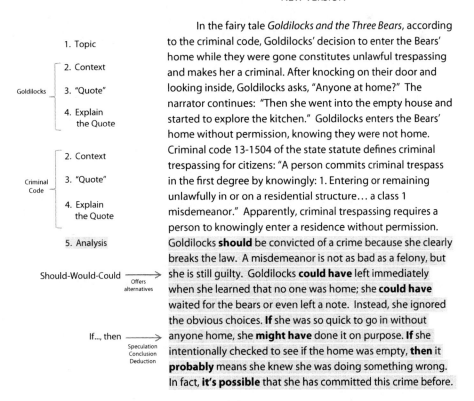

In the fairy tale *Goldilocks and the Three Bears*, according to the criminal code, Goldilocks' decision to enter the Bears' home while they were gone constitutes unlawful trespassing and makes her a criminal. After knocking on their door and looking inside, Goldilocks asks, "Anyone at home?" The narrator continues: "Then she went into the empty house and started to explore the kitchen." Goldilocks enters the Bears' home without permission, knowing they were not home. Criminal code 13-1504 of the state statute defines criminal trespassing for citizens: "A person commits criminal trespass in the first degree by knowingly: 1. Entering or remaining unlawfully in or on a residential structure... a class 1 misdemeanor." Apparently, criminal trespassing requires a person to knowingly enter a residence without permission. Goldilocks **should** be convicted of a crime because she clearly breaks the law. A misdemeanor is not as bad as a felony, but she is still guilty. Goldilocks **could have** left immediately when she learned that no one was home; she **could have** waited for the bears or even left a note. Instead, she ignored the obvious choices. **If** she was so quick to go in without anyone home, she **might have** done it on purpose. **If** she intentionally checked to see if the home was empty, **then** it **probably** means she knew she was doing something wrong. In fact, **it's possible** that she has committed this crime before.

Guided Practice: *Hatchet*, by Gary Paulsen

TEXT AND GOAL: Ms. Rios wants her students to write a literary analysis of Gary Paulsen's book *Hatchet*, but she needs to design a question that will allow her students to gather and organize evidence. From that evidence, they will then write a critical response, a paragraph with multiple quotations. Class discussion has explored two types of survival in the story: physical and emotional. She would love it if they could write about a physical symbol representing an emotional struggle.

Using the Map

Step 1: Ms. Rios wants to examine *Ideas & Content* of the text.

Step 2: She wants students to interpret the physical symbols of the text as they relate to protagonist Brian Robeson's emotional experience (*Comprehension*).

Step 3: She elects to use *Tool #4—Says This, Means That* (Symbol)—and Tool #6, *Find a Link* (Cause & Effect), to design her question.

CREATING THE QUESTION: In a few moments, Ms. Rios creates a question.

- In the book *Hatchet*, how does author Gary Paulsen use physical symbols to represent Brian Robeson's emotional experience? Support your answer. Consider the possible impact this might have on the reader.

She explains that "support your answer" usually means to find textual evidence. By adding the second piece—"consider the possible impact" and "on the reader"—Ms. Rios hopes to extend beyond comprehension into deeper-level thinking through *Cause & Effect* (speculation) and *Another's Point of View*. She writes the question on the board and passes out an Evidence Finder to each student.

FINDING EVIDENCE: To connect the *physical symbol* to the *emotional experience*, Ms. Rios knows her students need a minimum of two pieces of evidence. On a projected copy, Ms. Rios writes (as do students):

I want to find evidence of *a physical symbol that might represent Brian Robeson's emotional experience*.

Then Ms. Rios and her class focus on Brian's emotional struggle with his parents' divorce. While he struggles to survive in the woods after a plane crash, he often thinks of his parents. With a little guidance, students discover possible symbols, listing them on the board as they surface in discussion:

Figure 5.15 Symbolism in *Hatchet*

	Physical symbol	Emotional struggle
A	* Plane crashing	* Brian's life is crashing
B	* Wilderness survival	* Coming to terms with life
C	* Starting and keeping a fire	* Remembering his parents
D	* Gathering food	* Finding hope in knowledge

Ms. Rios takes a minute to have small groups **rank** their choices—ACDB or BADC, etc. (Tool #12)—based on the strength of the symbol. As expected, most groups have differing opinions, but evaluating the evidence makes for good critical thinking practice. For their paragraph together, students decide on letter C: the fire, accordingly determining their **topic**. Students present their first **evidence**:

Figure 5.16 Evidence Finder: Choosing a Topic

1 TOPIC	CONTEXT		QUOTE	EXPLAIN THE QUOTE	ANALYSIS
Physical fire = Parents	WHO	TO WHOM	"The sparks poured like a golden waterfall. At first they seemed to take…, but they all died (90)… He needed more, and more. He could not let the flames go out [again]" (92).		
	WHEN	WHERE			

Note the use of parentheses. Teachers who use MLA source citation can have students write their page numbers from the text, and this is a good opportunity to teach the rule. Also note the use of ellipses used here to show the omission of portions of the text, and brackets, used for clarification; the opportunity to demonstrate these three conventions could be a valuable teaching moment. Ms. Rios then asks students to help her find the **context**: "Who said this?" pointing to the green quote on her board. Students recognize author Gary Paulsen is speaking to the reader. Ms. Rios solicits the *when* and *where* from students to complete the context.

Figure 5.17 Evidence Finder: Identifying Context

1 TOPIC	CONTEXT		QUOTE	EXPLAIN THE QUOTE	ANALYSIS
Physical fire = Parents	WHO Author Gary Paulsen	TO WHOM Readers	"The sparks poured like a golden waterfall. At first they seemed to take…, but they all died (90)… [Brian] needed more, and more. He could not let the flames go out [again]" (92).	Here Paulsen—	
	WHEN After several attempts	WHERE Entrance to cave			

To **explain the quote**, Ms. Rios then reminds students that they can (but don't have to) begin with the word "Here" followed by the person speaking.

Ms. Rios: But, formal writing requires us to use the last name of the author.
Student: Paulsen.
Ms. Rios: Now I need a strong verb to describe what Mr. Paulsen is doing.
Student: Paulsen uses a simile—
Ms. Rios: To . . .?
Student: Describe the sparks.
Ms. Rios: Describes. Good, keep going. We want to use different words, strong words, to convey as much as we can of the original quote.

Figure 5.18 Evidence Finder: Explaining the Quote

Ms. Rios' class completes the explanation.

1 TOPIC	CONTEXT		QUOTE	EXPLAIN THE QUOTE	ANALYSIS
Physical fire = Parents	WHO Author Gary Paulsen	TO WHOM Readers	"The sparks poured like a golden waterfall. At first they seemed to take…, but they all died (90)… [Brian] needed more, and more. He could not let the flames go out [again]" (92).	Here Paulsen uses a simile to describe the radiant sparks that sadly extinguished. He is determined not to let the flames die again.	He is probably very frightened because he knows that if the fire goes out, he could die.
	WHEN After several attempts	WHERE Entrance to cave			

Now her class has a choice to make: they can **analyze** the first piece of evidence by itself or wait to draw conclusions till after the second piece of evidence. Ms. Rios offers a tool to help with the first option:

Tool #10

Another's Point of View

Ms. Rios: Let's use Tool #10, *Another's Point of View*. How might Brian be feeling at this point?

Student: He is probably very frightened because he knows that if the fire goes out, he could die.

Ms. Rios repeats the process for the second quote with the topic unchanged. Ms. Rios asks her class, "Help me make the connection between the symbol of fire and Brian's emotional struggle with his parents' divorce." **Key words** "it seems" help students articulate the connection.

Figure 5.19 Evidence Finder: Drawing a Conclusion

2 TOPIC	CONTEXT		QUOTE	EXPLAIN THE QUOTE	ANALYSIS
SAME	WHO Author	TO WHOM Reader	"And he thought, rolling thoughts, with the smoke curling up over his head… I wonder what my father is doing now. I wonder what my mother is doing now. I wonder if she is with him" (93).	Paulsen uses a metaphor to describe his thoughts floating up like smoke. His attention turns to his parents.	It seems Paulsen uses sparks to represent the feelings Brian's parents once had for each other, a flame he hopes will burn again.
	WHEN After success building a fire	WHERE Entrance to cave			

The Secret Recipe

Ms. Rios' class begins their baseline **multi-quote** paragraph by restating the question and the first topic box to create their claim. From there, Ms. Rios moves from left to right on the Evidence Finder. Then she repeats the process with her students for the second quote.

Figure 5.20 *Hatchet* Paragraph—Baseline Version

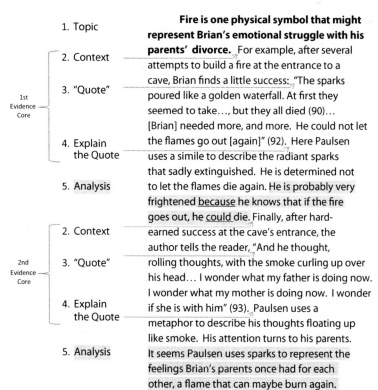

Teaching moment for students: When using a complete sentence to lead into a quotation, a colon is used. This is called a "formal introduction" to a quote, as opposed to a phrase or subordinate clause called an "informal introduction," which is followed by a comma. They select three tools to go deeper.

Critical Thinking Tools

Figure 5.21 Tool #4: Says This, Means That

Tool #4

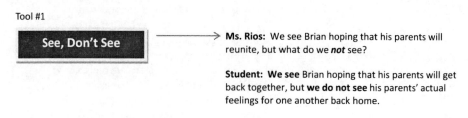

Ms. Rios: We've talked about the sparks potentially representing the parents' feelings for each other, and the flame their relationship. What could the author be **implying** about the smoke?

Student: It says in the text that Brian's thoughts were "rolling thoughts" like smoke.

Ms. Rios: So... what might the author be implying?

Student: Maybe Brian's thoughts will eventually disappear. I mean, they're only thoughts. Smoke doesn't control fire.

Ms. Rios: No matter what he might think he can't control—

Student: —his parents.

Figure 5.22 Tool #1: See, Don't See

Tool #1

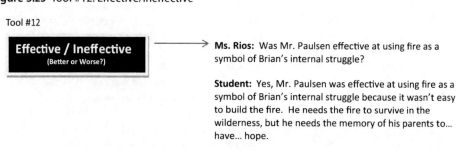

Ms. Rios: We see Brian hoping that his parents will reunite, but what do we *not* see?

Student: **We see** Brian hoping that his parents will get back together, but **we do not see** his parents' actual feelings for one another back home.

Figure 5.23 Tool #12: Effective/Ineffective

Tool #12

Effective / Ineffective
(Better or Worse?)

Ms. Rios: Was Mr. Paulsen effective at using fire as a symbol of Brian's internal struggle?

Student: Yes, Mr. Paulsen was effective at using fire as a symbol of Brian's internal struggle because it wasn't easy to build the fire. He needs the fire to survive in the wilderness, but he needs the memory of his parents to... have... hope.

With these responses, Ms. Rios' class is ready to deepen their paragraph:

Figure 5.24 *Hatchet* Paragraph—New Version

NEW VERSION

1st Evidence Core
1. Topic
2. Context
3. "Quote"
4. Explain the Quote
5. Analysis

2nd Evidence Core
2. Context
3. "Quote"
4. Explain the Quote
5. Analysis

Says this, Means that

See, Don't See

Effective-Ineffective

Fire is one physical symbol that might represent Brian's emotional struggle with his parents' divorce. For example, after several attempts to build a fire at the entrance to a cave, Brian finds a little success: "The sparks poured like a golden waterfall. At first they seemed to take…, but they all died (90)… [Brian] needed more, and more. He could not let the flames go out [again]" (92). Here Paulsen uses a simile to describe the radiant sparks that sadly extinguished. He is determined not to let the flames die again. Brian is probably very frightened because he knows that if the fire goes out, he could die. Finally, after hard-earned success at the cave's entrance, the author tells the reader, "And he thought, rolling thoughts, with the smoke curling up over his head… I wonder what my father is doing now. I wonder what my mother is doing now. I wonder if she is with him" (93). Paulsen uses a metaphor to describe Brian's thoughts floating up like smoke. His attention turns to his parents. It seems Paulsen uses sparks to represent the feelings Brian's parents once had for each other, a flame that can maybe burn again. Brian's thoughts were "rolling thoughts" **like smoke** and may eventually disappear. They're only thoughts. Smoke doesn't control fire. No matter what he might think or want, he can't control his parents. **We see** Brian hoping that his parents will get back together, **but we do not see** his parents' actual feelings for one another back home. Paulsen was **effective** at using fire as a symbol of Brian's internal struggle **because** it wasn't easy to build the fire. He needs the fire to survive in the wilderness, but he needs the memory of his parents to keep his hope alive.

Guided Practice: *The Giver*, by Lois Lowry

TEXT AND GOAL: In this dystopian story, young Jonas receives the assignment to be his community's "Receiver of Memories." Ms. Edens would like her students to examine the value of society's memories—good or bad—by using their own life experiences as a reference.

Using the Map

Step 1: Ms. Edens wants her students to examine **the text**, specifically the *Ideas and Content*.

Step 2: She wants them **to evaluate** Jonas and his community in some way using the evidence from the text *and* their own lives. Then she wants them **to construct** a claim and use evidence to defend it in a paragraph.

Step 3: She chooses *Tool #6*, "*Find a Link*," to connect the text with their own lives and *Tool #12*, "*Ranking*," to determine the best evidence to use to construct their claim.

CREATING THE QUESTION: Ms. Edens knows her question will have to be text-dependent yet invite students to respond using their personal experience as a lens. She arrives at two possible questions:

- What is it about Jonas' society that makes eliminating potential harm so harmful?
- Which of Jonas' received memories is the most disturbing based on your own experience? Why?

Ms. Edens determines that the first question, while appropriate, might semantically confuse a few of her lower-level students. She opts for the clarity of the second one: she reasons, by having her students rank what they believe are Jonas' most disturbing memories and respond critically to one of them through their own experience, she will invite higher-level thinking.

FINDING EVIDENCE: To prepare her students to select the best evidence, she has them prepare a simple T-chart, which will allow her students to list Jonas' received memories on the left side and their respective (and varied) firsthand experiences on the right. By making a list, the process constitutes analysis; by ranking them in order of most disturbing, the process constitutes evaluation.

Figure 5.25 Compare T-Chart—*The Giver*

Received Memories	Personal Experiences
* Sledding accident	* Wrecked my bike
* War	* Dad served in military
* Family holiday	* Christmas with grandparents
* Color	* Sunset

When Ms. Edens reiterates her question, at first the class immediately responds that "war" would be the most "disturbing" because of its graphic nature and subsequent pain that it inflicts on Jonas as he receives memory of it—until they realize this society does *not* have war, a condition that is *not* (at least ostensibly) disturbing. Students next gravitate toward a physical accident like a sledding accident, only to arrive at the same realization: this society has eliminated such painful experiences. And how can *that* be disturbing? Students could not relate to seeing life in black and white, except for a few who had seen old movies and a reference to blindness. A society void of all color would definitely be disturbing. But after discussion, students determine that while the memory of the family holiday given to Jonas was warm and inviting, a society's life without a real family would be most disturbing.

I want to find evidence of *the most disturbing memory Jonas received based on my own experience.*

Family holiday then becomes the topic, or something like *No family holiday is sad* becomes the claim. Students provide the quotation they selected from the text and take turns providing the context boxes as Ms. Edens asks the questions: *Who said "Warmth . . . and happiness. . . ?"* Then: *"To whom was Jonas talking?"* And so on. She helps them explain what Jonas was saying, and together they fill in the box. The question "Why is this disturbing?" prompts their reasoning in the analysis box.

Figure 5.26 Evidence Finder: Choosing a Topic

The Giver

1	TOPIC	CONTEXT		QUOTE	EXPLAIN THE QUOTE	ANALYSIS
	Family holiday	WHO	TO WHOM	"Warmth …and happiness. And—let me think. *Family*. That it was a celebration of some sort, a holiday… I like the feeling of love… [but] I can see that it was a dangerous way to live."	Jonas does not have a real family. He experiences a memory of one and is not sure why the feeling frightens him.	It is very sad that Jonas does not know the feeling of love that a family can provide. It's very disturbing that he thinks it's dangerous.
		Jonas	The Giver			
		WHEN	WHERE			
		After receiving memory	Annex room			

Personal Experience

2	TOPIC	CONTEXT		EXPERIENCE	ANALYSIS
	Christmas with grand-parent	WHO WAS THERE		Like Jonas' memory, my holiday experience had packages to unwrap, gifts that included toys, clothes, and other items. We also had lights and decorations around the room. We laughed and hugged, thanking each other for the presents. Then we had breakfast together as a family.	This time with my family brought me "warmth" like Jonas described, and it would be lonely without them— or without that feeling.
		Grandparents, Mom & Dad, Aunt Caroline, my older sisters			
		WHEN	WHERE		
		Last December	Grand-parents' home		

For their personal experience, the topic is really the *event*. The context is very similar: *Who was there? When did it happen? Where?* Students then write a brief anecdote that relates to Jonas' experience. Students can use the backs of their Evidence Finders if needed, but a few sentences carefully selected should suffice. If their anecdote includes dialogue (which is a quote), even better: simply have students use it the same way they do with quotes from a text. The analysis then articulates the connection.

Students are then ready to write a baseline paragraph. Using Mrs. Edens' question and their first topic (or claim) box, they can write their first sentence. Students help Mrs. Edens write a piece at a time on the board. More independent students will begin to use their own phrasing.

Figure 5.27 *The Giver* Paragraph—Baseline Version

	THE SECRET RECIPE	BASELINE EXAMPLE
The Giver	1. **Topic (or Claim)** 2. Context 3. "Quote" 4. Explain the Quote 5. Analysis	**Based on my own experience, strangely the most disturbing memory Jonas received was one of a family holiday.** After receiving the memory in the Annex room from the Giver, Jonas says to him, "Warmth… and happiness. And—let me think. *Family*. That it was a celebration of some sort, a holiday… I like the feeling of love… [but] I can see that it was a *dangerous way to live.*" Jonas does not have a real family. He experiences a memory of one and is not sure why the feeling frightens him. It is very sad that Jonas does not know the feeling of love a family can provide. It's very disturbing that he thinks it's dangerous.
Personal Experience	1. **Topic (or Claim)** 2. Context 3. "Quote" (experience) 4. Explain the Quote (skipped) 5. Analysis	**I have had a family holiday also, a Christmas with my grandparents.** Last December my parents and sisters, along with my aunt Caroline, and I visited my grandparents in Denver, Colorado. Like Jonas' memory, my holiday experience had packages to unwrap, gifts that included toys, clothes, and other items. We also had lights and decorations around the room. We laughed and hugged, thanking each other for the presents. Then we had breakfast together as a family. This time with my family brought me "warmth" like Jonas described, and it would be lonely without them—or without that feeling.

With this baseline paragraph (or two paragraphs if split at the second topic), Ms. Edens has helped her students write a solid response and now wants to see how the critical thinking tools might deepen that response. Using her own tool sheet for teachers, she selects a few that seem to apply with her subject. She prepares a few initial questions in advance and projects them onto the board; students use their version of the same tool sheet to help them respond if they need it.

Critical Thinking Tools

Figure 5.28 Tool #4: Says This, Means That

Tool #4

Says This, Means That
Figurative Language   Symbol   Inference

→ **Ms. Edens:** When Jonas uses the word "dangerous" to describe the family setting, **what can be inferred?**

Student: When Jonas uses the word "dangerous" to describe the family setting, it can be inferred that love scares Jonas.

Ms. Edens: What do you mean?

Student: The feeling was new for him. Anything new can be scary.

Ms. Edens: True, but he likes the feeling. How can that be scary?

Student: Maybe he's afraid he will lose it. Or he is starting to realize what he has been missing.

Figure 5.29 Tool #9: Another's Point of View

Tool #9

Another's Point of View

→ **Ms. Edens:** How might **Jonas' parents feel** if he was to describe for them his experience?

Student: Nothing. They don't feel anything. I mean, they're not his real parents anyway. They wouldn't understand.

Ms. Edens: And how might that make Jonas feel, that they wouldn't understand?

Student: All alone.

Ms. Edens: You mean *isolated*. Why?

Student: He won't be able to explain this new feeling to anyone, and it's probably frightening to feel like you can't communicate.

While a single paragraph is acceptable, the added analysis prompts Ms. Edens' class to split the single paragraph into two paragraphs: one for Jonas' experience and one for his or her own. Their use of the Critical Thinking Tools deepens both analyses.

Figure 5.30 *The Giver* Paragraph—New Version

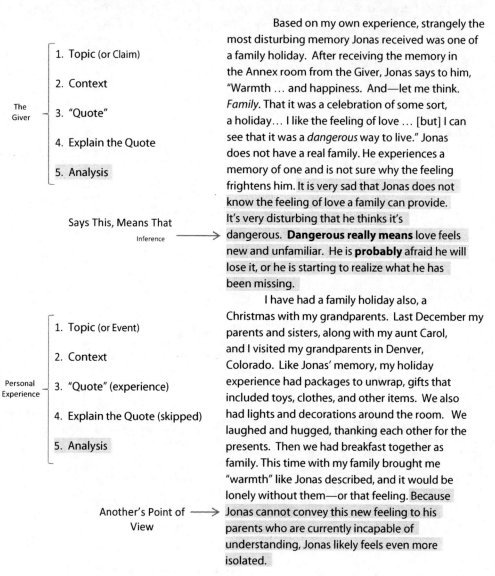

Gettysburg Address, by Abraham Lincoln

TEXT AND GOAL: Mr. Johnson's class has been studying President Abraham Lincoln's *Gettysburg Address* from the Civil War. In class they have been also learning about literary devices like tone, mood, parallelism, and others. Mr. Johnson wants to design a text-dependent question that will invite his students to consider how Lincoln's literary techniques might have impacted his audience.

Using the Map

Step 1: Mr. Johnson wants his students to **examine the text**, specifically Lincoln's **voice**, which is to examine "how" the author developed his tone. Specifically, Johnson wants his students to understand why Lincoln used such a tone with his audience.

Step 2: He wants students to consider the *possible impact* Lincoln's technique(s) might have had on listeners, which is **analysis,** specifically a *Tool #5 Find a Link: Cause & Effect*. The exercise will help him connect the dots, so to speak.

Step 3: The moment Mr. Johnson asks his students to select a possible impact and defend it by using evidence and their own reasoning, he is asking his students to **create** a **claim** and defend it. Examples of Lincoln's **tone** within the text will comprise students' evidence, and the possible impact of those words will become their elaboration.

CREATING THE QUESTION: Mr. Johnson arrives at a couple options.

- In the *Gettysburg Address*, what impact will Abraham Lincoln's tone likely have upon its listeners?
- What literary devices does Abraham Lincoln use in his *Gettysburg Address*? How do those tools help him accomplish his purpose?

Mr. Johnson's second question is very effective and may allow for an examination of multiple literary devices, but he has not taught literary devices or figurative language before. He opts for the first question but wants to pursue the second one in a collaborative effort with a language arts teacher in the future. He may also use select cue cards in Chapter 7 of this book prior to his teaching the *Gettysburg Address*.

Evidence Finder

Mr. Johnson projects his evidence finder onto the board and writes his question off to the side. Using the question students are able to help their teacher fill out the top portion of the organizer, which they record on their respective copies:

> I want to find evidence of *Abraham Lincoln's tone in his Gettysburg Address.*

TOPIC (or Claim): Before recording the evidence, Mr. Johnson asks his students to help him list distinct tones they notice in the text. Each time a student offers a possibility, Mr. Johnson writes the example on the board, asking, "Will you read us the line that makes you think that way?" Several good examples come out of the discussion, including humble, grateful, reverent, serious, respectful, and patriotic. Students choose the first one, *humble* or *humility*. Mr. Johnson then asks them to find a quote from the text that demonstrates President Lincoln's humility.

They decide on a **QUOTE** and write it in the *Evidence Finder*:

Figure 5.31 Evidence Finder: Choosing a Topic

TOPIC	CONTEXT		QUOTE	EXPLAIN THE QUOTE	ANALYSIS
Humble	**WHO** President Lincoln	**TO WHOM** Parents of fallen soldiers	"But in a larger sense, we can not dedicate— we can not hallow— this ground. The brave men, living and dead, who struggled here, have consecrated it, far above our poor power to add or detract."		
	WHEN Four months after battle	**WHERE** Field at Gettysburg, PA			

CONTEXT: Mr. Johnson knows that the context of this evidence is very important in this particular event. He hopes they will give a little more detail given his previous lesson. Mr. Johnson begins: "*Who* said the quote is easy: President Lincoln. But do you remember *to whom* President Lincoln was speaking?" Students take turns explaining that Lincoln's audience included heartbroken Americans from the north and south. Whether in the immediate sound of his voice or in the newspapers shortly thereafter, Lincoln's listeners or readers would include parents and other family members of fallen soldiers who would be in attendance. Students recall that it was only *four months earlier* that the battle had been fought *on the very ground* where the speech was now being delivered.

Explaining the quote takes practice, but it is a very important skill. Mr. Johnson starts them off with "Here, the president . . . " After a few attempts, they opt for the verb "acknowledges," and complete the box:

Figure 5.32 Evidence Finder: Identifying Context and Explaining the Quote

TOPIC	CONTEXT		QUOTE	EXPLAIN THE QUOTE	ANALYSIS
Humble	WHO President Lincoln	TO WHOM Parents of fallen soldiers	"But in a larger sense, we can not dedicate—we can not hallow—this ground. The brave men, living and dead, who struggled here, have consecrated it, far above our poor power to add or detract."	Here Lincoln acknowledges his own inability to make the ground holy, giving credit to the men who fought there instead.	
	WHEN Four months after battle	WHERE Field at Gettysburg, PA			

To fill out the analysis portion, Mr. Johnson reiterates the question, which is to determine how Lincoln's tone may have impacted his audience, a Cause and Effect question. Tool #6 should help his students complete the Evidence Finder. He draws a dot-to-dot on the board representing the situation.

Tool #6

Figure 5.33 Tool #6: Find a Link

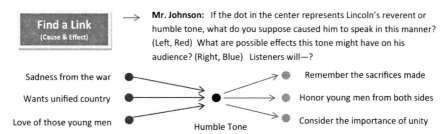

Mr. Johnson: If the dot in the center represents Lincoln's reverent or humble tone, what do you suppose caused him to speak in this manner? (Left, Red) What are possible effects this tone might have on his audience? (Right, Blue) Listeners will—?

Even this one tool is enough to complete the final box preparatory to completing the paragraph:

Figure 5.34 Evidence Finder: Drawing a Conclusion—*I want to find evidence of Abraham Lincoln's tone in his Gettysburg Address.*

TOPIC	CONTEXT		QUOTE	EXPLAIN THE QUOTE	ANALYSIS
Humble	WHO President Lincoln	TO WHOM Parents of fallen soldiers	"But in a larger sense, we can not dedicate—we can not hallow—this ground. The brave men, living and dead, who struggled here, have consecrated it, far above our poor power to add or detract."	Here Lincoln acknowledges his own inability to make the ground holy, giving credit to the men who fought there instead.	By using his reverent tone, Lincoln's listeners will likely remember the great sacrifices these young made in giving their lives.
	WHEN Four months after battle	WHERE Field at Gettysburg, PA			

The Secret Recipe

Mr. Johnson writes The Secret Recipe along the left side of the board and leaves room on the right to craft the sample. To get started, he uses the "I want to find evidence of" line and the Topic box to write to help students draft the claim.

Figure 5.35 *Gettysburg Address* Paragraph—Baseline Version

BASELINE PARAGRAPH

1. **Topic** (or Claim)
2. **Context**
3. **"Quote"**
4. **Explain the Quote**
5. **Analysis**

In his speech "The Gettysburg Address," President Abraham Lincoln uses a humble tone to impact his listeners. Giving the speech four months after the battle on the very field where soldiers lost their lives in Gettysburg, Pennsylvania, President Lincoln speaks to a group of dedicated Americans, including parents and family members of fallen soldiers, saying, "But in a larger sense, we can not dedicate—we can not hallow—this ground. The brave men, living and dead, who struggled here, have consecrated it, far above our poor power to add or detract." Here Lincoln acknowledges his own inability to make the ground holy, giving credit to the men who fought there instead. **By using his reverent tone, Lincoln's listeners will likely remember the great sacrifices these young made in giving their lives.**

Students write the paragraph, also. They retrieve their 12 Tools page and from it determine which tools might work to enhance their paragraph. Mr. Johnson facilitates as needed:

Figure 5.36 Critical Thinking Tools

Tool #1

See, Don't See

→ **Mr. Johnson:** We see Lincoln referring to the "brave men, living and dead." But what do we *not* see?

Student: We see Lincoln referring to "brave men, living and dead," but we do not see him referring to northern boys or southern boys.

Tool #10

Another's Point of View

→ **Mr. Johnson:** And how might his audience respond to his reverence for boys on both sides?

Student: Parents would appreciate his respect for them.

Mr. Johnson: If you had lost a son?

Student: I would be really sad.

Mr. Johnson: If you had lost a *Confederate* son, and you were listening to a Union president?—would that change the way you feel?

Figure 5.36 Continued

Student: Even if I disagreed with him on the war, I would really appreciate his, his...

Mr. Johnson: Reverence?

Student: Yeah, reverence for my son. I would remember that respect, even if we were to lose the war. I wouldn't want my son forgotten.

Tool #8

→ **Mr. Johnson:** Would Lincoln's audience have perceived the speech differently, if he had only mentioned northern sons?

Student: I think if Lincoln would have mentioned only northern sons, his southern listeners would have ignored his message about unifying the country.

While much more could be said using each tool, Mr. Johnson's class now has enough to enhance their paragraph critically. He returns to the baseline paragraph they have constructed.

Figure 5.37 *Gettysburg Address* Paragraph—Baseline Version

NEW VERSION

1. Topic

2. Context

3. "Quote"

4. Explain the Quote

5. Analysis

See, Don't See →

Others' Points of View →

If...Then →
Should-Would-Could
Change
Link: Cause and Effect

In his speech "The Gettysburg Address," President Abraham Lincoln uses a humble tone to impact his listeners. Giving the speech four months after the battle on the very field where soldiers lost their lives in Gettysburg, Pennsylvania, President Lincoln speaks to a group of dedicated Americans, including parents and family members of fallen soldiers, saying, "But in a larger sense, we can not dedicate—we can not consecrate—we can not hallow—this ground. The brave men, living and dead, who struggled here, have consecrated it, far above our poor power to add or detract." Here Lincoln acknowledges his own inability to make the ground holy, giving credit to the men who fought there instead. By using his reverent tone, Lincoln's listeners will likely remember the great sacrifices these young made in giving their lives. Lincoln intentionally refers to 'brave men, living and dead,' **but does not refer** to northern boys or southern boys. **Parents from both sides** would have appreciated his respect for their sons. Even Confederate **mothers** would have appreciated the reverence he showed for their sons. After all, they don't want their sons forgotten any more than northern mothers. **If** he **would** have only mentioned northern sons, **his tone would have changed**, and his southern listeners **might have ignored his message** about unifying the country.

Notice how the tools overlap and merge. They're really not meant to be discrete methods, but to serve as sentence starters for young people who will gradually become more comfortable making deeper-level comments in succession. Also, students familiar with additional literary devices—parallelism (in this instance, anaphora), dashes, and alliteration, for example—could offer additional insight on the evidence, with respect to tone:

Cause and Effect → **By using anaphora**, a type of parallelism where the repeated lines begin the same and end differently, saying "we can not dedicate—we can not hallow," Lincoln is able to be both emphatic and humble at the same time. **By using dashes**, he draws attention to his most important point, his own insignificance in making the ground sacred. **By using alliteration**, "poor power," Lincoln adds a melodic aspect to his fluency, adding a softening beauty to his tone.

Optional Scaffolding

If you discover that your students are struggling with "explaining the quote," that is to paraphrase the text so as to demonstrate comprehension, you may consider making for students an additional scaffold prior to the Evidence Finder; see Figure 5.38 as an example. Separating the excerpts into smaller pieces seems to help remove some of the intimidation, especially for more complex texts.

Figure 5.38 *Gettysburg Address*—Scaffolding Worksheet

Name: _____

Comprehension: Gettysburg Address

At the dedication of the Soldiers' National Cemetery in Gettysburg, Pennsylvania, four months after the great American Civil War battle there cost the lives of roughly 5,600 soldiers, President Abraham Lincoln delivered the following address on November 19, 1863.

Directions: Explain each excerpt using one or more complete sentences in adjacent the right.

QUOTE	EXPLAIN THE QUOTE
"Four score and seven years ago our fathers brought forth on this continent, a new nation, conceived in Liberty, and dedicated to the proposition that all men are created equal.	
"Now we are engaged in a great civil war, testing whether that nation, or any nation so conceived and so dedicated, can long endure.	
"We are met on a great battle-field of that war. We have come to dedicate a portion of that field, as a final resting place for those who here gave their lives that that nation might live. It is altogether fitting that we should do this.	
"But, in a larger sense, we can not dedicate—we can not consecrate—we can not hallow—this ground. The brave men, living and dead, who struggled here, have consecrated it, far above our poor power to add or detract.	

Figure 5.38 Continued

"The world will little note, nor long remember what we say here, but it can never forget what they did here.

"It is for us the living, rather, to be dedicated here to the unfinished work which they who fought here have thus far so nobly advanced.

"It is rather for us to be here dedicated to the great task remaining before us—that from these honored dead we take increased devotion to that cause for which they gave the last full measure of devotion—

"—that we here highly resolve that these dead shall not have died in vain—that this nation, under God, shall have a new birth of freedom—

"—and that government of the people, by the people, for the people, shall not perish from the earth."

6

Extra Examples Using Mentor Texts

Unlike Chapter 5 that gives more step-by-step instructions as guided practice for teachers, Chapter 6 is meant to provide similar but more abridged examples of literary analyses using a cross-section of texts—canonical, popular, and seminal/historical texts—common to upper elementary and middle schools. Whether part of an essay or short answer, examples offer something of a variety.

Questions below may help you design a prompt with a similar focus, even if you are using a different piece of literature. Or they may serve as visual illustrations for students.

Figure 6.1 Sample Text Prompts

Text	Author	Question or Prompt	Focus
The Adventures of Tom Sawyer	Mark Twain	Twain writes in Chapter 2: "In order to make a man or a boy covet a thing, it is only necessary to make the thing difficult to attain." How might this have been true for Tom? How might this be true for you?	Application (Text to Self)
Bud, Not Buddy	Christopher Paul Curtis	How can nicknames change a person? Use evidence from the text to support your answer.	Cause and Effect
Declaration of Independence	Thomas Jefferson	How is The Declaration of Independence organized, and how might this have affected King George's reaction?	Organization / Cause and Effect
Ender's Game	Orson Scott Card	Is Ender more like his brother Peter or more like his sister Valentine?	Compare / Contrast
Holes	Louis Sachar	How does the author use conventions to enhance his story?	Conventions
Inaugural Address, 1961	John F. Kennedy	Kennedy refers more than once to the atomic bomb. What does he propose as a solution to this national fear? Do you agree or disagree with Kennedy's viewpoint?	Agree or Disagree
Letter from Birmingham Jail	Martin Luther King, Jr.	How does King feel about creating tension? Do you agree or disagree? Why?	Agree or Disagree
Narrative of the Life of Frederick Douglass: An American Slave	Frederick Douglass	How does becoming literate—learning to read—affect Frederick Douglass?	Cause and Effect
		How does Douglass use literary devices to develop his theme of literacy being life-changing?	Literary Devices / Theme
The Star Spangled Banner	Francis Scott Key	How do lyrics from the Star Spangled Banner reflect early American values? Are those values shared today?	Correlation
Stargirl	Jerry Spinelli	How is Stargirl different from normal teenagers? Is it wise for her to be this way?	Compare / Contrast
The Outsiders	S.E. Hinton	How does the author use the color gold to develop her theme?	Symbol / Theme
The Ransom of Red Chief	O. Henry	How does O. Henry's use irony to develop his story, "The Ransom of Red Chief"?	Irony / Cause & Effect
To Kill a Mockingbird	Harper Lee	What can we learn from Atticus in the way he treats others? Use evidence from the text to support your answer.	Character
Tuck Everlasting	Natalie Babbitt	Did Winnie make the right decision refusing to drink the water that would make her immortal? Use evidence to support your answer.	Agree or Disagree
The Watsons Go to Birmingham—1963	Christopher Paul Curtis	Using Byron's fight with Larry Dunn as your focus, when does self-defense (or exacting justice) become bullying?	Evaluation

Figure 6.2 Evidence Finder 3.0—*Narrative of the Life of Frederick Douglass: An American Slave*

Narrative of the Life of Frederick Douglass: An American Slave
Written by Himself

I want to find evidence of how learning to read, or literacy, affected Frederick Douglass.

1 TOPIC	CONTEXT		QUOTE	EXPLAIN THE QUOTE	ANALYSIS
Example or Claim Gains awareness of human rights	WHO Douglass	TO WHOM Possibly literate whites	"What I got from Sheridan was a bold denunciation of slavery, and a powerful vindication of human rights. The reading of these documents enabled me to utter my thoughts, and to meet the arguments brought forward to sustain slavery" (50).	Douglas learned the value of human rights and for the first time could express his reasons to oppose slavery.	**Elaboration or Rationale** If Douglass had not learned to read, he would likely have remained ignorant of civil rights. Reading gave Douglass a voice he didn't have before.
	WHEN After learning to read	WHERE Hugh's family home			

2 TOPIC	CONTEXT		QUOTE	EXPLAIN THE QUOTE	ANALYSIS
Example or Claim Now hates enslavers	WHO Douglass	TO WHOM Readers familiar with slavery	"The more I read, the more I was led to abhor and detest my enslavers" (51).	Gradually, Douglass began to hate all who enslaved him and others like him.	**Elaboration or Rationale** Reading had an effect upon Douglass' perception of slave owners. For the first time, he probably began to see their selfishness and greed.
	WHEN Upon reading "Columbian Orator"	WHERE Auto-biography			

3 TOPIC	CONTEXT		QUOTE	EXPLAIN THE QUOTE	ANALYSIS
Example or Claim Experiences emotional suffering	WHO Douglass	TO WHOM Possibly literate whites	"It had given me a view of my wretched condition, without the remedy… In moments of agony, I envied my fellow slaves for their stupidity… It was this everlasting thinking of my condition that tormented me" (51).	Douglass felt deep sorrow when he became aware of his situation without a way to fix it.	**Elaboration or Rationale** Literacy showed Douglass alternatives to slavery, and when he could not have them, he hurt inside.
	WHEN After reading extensively	WHERE As a young boy in Maryland			

108 ◆ Extra Examples Using Mentor Texts

Figure 6.3 Evidence Finder 1.0—*Narrative of the Life of Frederick Douglass: An American Slave*

EVIDENCE FINDER 1.0

Narrative of the Life of Frederick Douglass: An American Slave
Written by Himself

From Evidence Finder on Page 107.

I want to find evidence of how learning to read, or literacy, affected Frederick Douglass.

3	TOPIC	CONTEXT		QUOTE	EXPLAIN THE QUOTE	ANALYSIS
	Experiences emotional suffering	WHO	TO WHOM	"It had given me a view of my wretched condition, without the remedy… In moments of agony, I envied my fellow slaves for their stupidity… It was this everlasting thinking of my condition that tormented me" (51).	Douglass felt deep sorrow when he became aware of his situation without a way to fix it.	Literacy showed Douglass alternatives to slavery, and when he could not have them, he hurt inside.
		Douglass	Possibly literate whites			
		WHEN	WHERE			
		After learning to read	As a young boy in Maryland			

BASELINE EXAMPLE

Topic ————— **One way learning to read affected Douglass was that it caused him great**

Context ————— **personal suffering emotionally.** Possibly speaking to literate whites supportive of his cause or to those undecided on the issue of slavery, Douglas explains that after learning the alphabet and reading secretly while living in the Hugh's family home, "What I got from Sheridan was a bold denunciation of slavery, and a

Quote ————— powerful vindication of human rights. The reading of these documents enabled me to utter my thoughts, and to meet the arguments brought forward to sustain slavery" (50). Douglas learned the value of human rights and for the first time

Explain the Quote ————— could express his reasons to oppose slavery. If Douglass had not learned to read, then it is likely he would have remained ignorant of civil rights.

Analysis ————— Reading gave Douglass a voice he didn't have before.

Figure 6.4 Evidence Finder 3.0—*Narrative of the Life of Frederick Douglass: An American Slave*

EVIDENCE FINDER 3.0 **Narrative of the Life of Frederick Douglass: An American Slave**
Written by Himself

I want to find evidence of <u>how Douglass uses a literary device to develop his theme of literacy being life-changing.</u>

1 TOPIC	CONTEXT		QUOTE	EXPLAIN THE QUOTE	ANALYSIS
Example or Claim: Parallelism	WHO	TO WHOM	"I saw nothing without seeing it, I heard nothing without hearing it, and I felt nothing without feeling it" (52).	Here Douglass uses parallelism to describe how it was impossible for him to see, hear, or feel anything without thinking of freedom.	Using parallelism helps Douglass emphasize his discovery. Learning to read has filled his thoughts with wonder.
	Douglass	Those yearning for freedom			
	WHEN	WHERE			
	After reading about the ills of slavery	In the "Columbian Orator"			

2 TOPIC	CONTEXT		QUOTE	EXPLAIN THE QUOTE	ANALYSIS
Example or Claim: Personification	WHO	TO WHOM	"It looked from every star, it smiled in every calm, it breathed in every wind, and moved in every storm" (52).	Douglass uses human functions like "looked," "smiled," and "moved" to personify freedom.	Using personification, Douglass makes freedom sound like a friend, someone who is both near us and always there for us.
	Douglass	Those who appreciate freedom			
	WHEN	WHERE			
	After using parallelism	In the next sentence			

3 TOPIC	CONTEXT		QUOTE	EXPLAIN THE QUOTE	ANALYSIS
Example or Claim: Metaphor	WHO	TO WHOM	"The silver trump of freedom had roused my soul to eternal wakefulness" (51-52).	Douglass uses a form of figurative language, a metaphor, to compare his awakening to the bright sound of a trumpet.	By using the metaphor, he creates an image of a musician playing his trumpet in the early morning something important.
	Douglass	Possibly literate whites			
	WHEN	WHERE			
	At the beginning of epiphany	As a young boy in Maryland			

Figure 6.5 *Narrative of the Life of Frederick Douglass: An American Slave*—Sample Essay

Narrative of the Life of Frederick Douglass: An American Slave
Written by Himself

Question: *How does Frederick Douglas use literary devices to develop his theme?*

How Literacy Affected Frederick Douglass

During his lifetime, former slave and respected statesman Frederick Douglass experienced harsh realities during this dark period in America history. In his autobiography, he relates how learning to read affected his life. He uses literary devices to develop literacy as one of his central themes.

[Topic] **One literary device Douglass uses to develop his theme of literacy being life-changing is parallelism.** [Context] After reading about the ills of slavery in a publication called "The Columbian Orator," Douglass is truly affected by it. He seems to write to those yearning for freedom when he says, [Quote] "I saw nothing without seeing it, I heard nothing without hearing it, and I felt nothing without feeling it" (52). [Explain the Quote] Here Douglas uses parallelism—which is to use the same structure in writing—to describe how it was impossible for him to see, hear, or feel anything without thinking of freedom. [Analysis] Clearly, learning to read has **filled his thoughts** with wonder. Using parallelism helps Douglass emphasize this discovery. [If..., then...] **If** Douglass **would** have simply stated that he appreciated freedom, without using parallelism to do it, then his approach may not have had as much impact on his audience. [Cause & Effect] His use of epistrophe, a type of parallelism in which repeated lines are structured to end the same way, **gives** a **sense of strength** to his conviction. It **likely causes** his reader **to appreciate his discovery**.

Douglass also uses personification to strengthen his belief in the power of literacy. In the next sentence Douglass addresses those who appreciate freedom, saying, "It looked from every star, it smiled in every calm, it breathed in every wind, and moved in every storm" (52). Douglass uses human

Figure 6.6 Evidence Finder 3.0—*The Outsiders*

EVIDENCE FINDER 3.0

The Outsiders
S.E. Hinton

I want to find evidence of <u>Hinton's use of the color gold to develop her theme.</u>

1 TOPIC	CONTEXT		QUOTE	EXPLAIN THE QUOTE	ANALYSIS
Example or Claim Gold as a new beginning	WHO	TO WHOM	"The clouds changed from gray to pin, the mist was touched with gold. There was a silent moment when everything held its breath, and then the sun rose. It was beautiful" (77).	Ponyboy uses personification— the morning "held its breath"—to emphasize the beauty of a golden sun at dawn.	Gold seems to represent the birth of a new morning, something that removes the darker clouds like the pain they are feeling.
	Ponyboy as narrator	Reader			
	WHEN	WHERE			
	Hiding from authorities	In the abandoned church			

2 TOPIC	CONTEXT		QUOTE	EXPLAIN THE QUOTE	ANALYSIS
Example or Claim Gold as temporary beauty	WHO	TO WHOM	"Nature's first green is gold / Her hardest hue to hold… So dawn goes down to day. Nothing gold can stay (77).	Frost seems to say that nature changes colors each season. Even beautiful colors fade.	Ponyboy wishes he could keep the morning colors, maybe even paint what he sees. He seems helpless as moments are fleeting.
	Ponyboy citing Robert Frost	Johnny			
	WHEN	WHERE			
	After the sunrise	On the porch			

3 TOPIC	CONTEXT		QUOTE	EXPLAIN THE QUOTE	ANALYSIS
Example or Claim Gold as innocence	WHO	TO WHOM	"Stay gold, Ponyboy. Stay gold…" (148).	Johnny wants Ponyboy to stay golden, probably alluding to Frost's poem.	This suggests Johnny more than anything else wants Ponyboy to hold onto his innocence as impossible as it might seem.
	Johnny	Ponyboy			
	WHEN	WHERE			
	Right before Johnny dies	In the hospital			

Figure 6.7 *The Outsiders*—Sample Essay

The Outsiders
S.E. Hinton

Question: *How does S.E. Hinton use the color to develop her theme?*

How Color Develops Theme

In her novel The Outsiders, S.E. Hinton regularly uses color, like the colors of characters' eyes, for example, to portray individuals' personalities or even foreshadow events. Most interestingly, though, she uses color—the color gold, specifically—to develop her theme of appreciating beauty and staying innocent during difficult times.

[Topic] [Context] **Gold first represents something of a new beginning.** While hiding from authorities in an abandoned church, Ponyboy (as narrator) tells the reader, [Quote] "The clouds changed from gray to pin, the mist was touched with gold. There was a silent moment when everything held its breath, and then the sun rose. It was beautiful" (77). [Explain the Quote] Through her character Ponyboy, Hinton uses personification—the morning "held its breath"—to emphasize the beauty of a golden sun at dawn. [Analysis] Compared to dark clouds, gold is bright and cheerful. The **color seems to represent** the birth of [Says This, Means That] a new morning, something that removes the darker clouds like the pain Ponyboy and Johnny are experiencing. Ponyboy and Johnny need a new beginning more than ever. [Another's Point of View] **They are likely feeling scared, alone, and hopeless.** Running from the authorities for potential murder has left them sensitive to beauty around them. A new golden sunrise (especially [Should-Would-Could] watching from a church) **could** be reminding them hope is still available.

Hinton deepens the idea that beauty is present but through the same color adds that beauty may only be temporary. Moments later after the sun rises, Ponyboy cites the poet Robert Frost to his friend Johnny: "Nature's first green is gold, / Her hardest hue to hold… / So dawn goes down to day. / Nothing gold can stay" (77). Frost seems to say that nature changes colors each season. Even beautiful colors fade. Ponyboy wishes he could enjoy his youth longer but knows he must grow up.

Figure 6.8 Evidence Finder 1.0—*To Kill a Mockingbird*

EVIDENCE FINDER 1.0

To Kill a Mockingbird
Harper Lee

I want to find evidence of <u>character attributes that define Atticus in Harper Lee's novel "To Kill a Mockingbird."</u>

1 TOPIC	CONTEXT		QUOTE	EXPLAIN THE QUOTE	ANALYSIS
Example or Claim Understanding person	WHO	TO WHOM	"Mr. Cunningham's basically a good man. He just has his blind spots along with the rest of us... He might have hurt me a little, but son, you'll understand folks a little better when you're older." (157).	Atticus recognizes that Mr. Cunningham wanted to hurt him physically, but he teaches Jem that Mr. Cunningham is essentially a good person.	Atticus could have thought poorly of Mr. Cunningham, but instead he humbly shares his belief that all men have "blind spots," something he sees in himself.
	Atticus	Jem			
	WHEN	WHERE			
	After a threat on his life	Speaking at the dinner table			

Topic — In **To Kill a Mockingbird**, author Harper Lee creates a character, Atticus,
who treats others in ways we can emulate. One attribute includes an

Context — **understanding heart.** One evening while speaking at the dinner table, after a
man named Mr. Cunningham had threatened him, Atticus tells Jem, "Mr.

Quote — Cunningham's basically a good man. He just has his blind spots along with the
rest of us. . . He might have hurt me a little, but son, you'll understand folks

Explain the Quote — a little better when you're older" (157). Atticus recognizes that Mr.
Cunningham wanted to hurt him physically, but instead he teaches Jem that Mr.
Cunningham is essentially a good person. Atticus **could have** thought poorly of

Analysis → Mr. Cunningham, but he chose to believe that all men have "blind spots,"

Should-Would-Could — something he sees in himself. Most people **would have** said something negative
about Mr. Cunningham. Atticus is able to truly understand another man's

Find a Link: Cause & Effect — perspective. I should slow down when I speak. This will allow me to
consider what others are thinking and feeling.

Figure 6.9 Evidence Finder 2.0—*Ender's Game*

EVIDENCE FINDER 2.0

Ender's Game
Orson Scott Card

I want to find evidence of <u>Ender acting like his brother Peter (and/or sister, Valentine).</u>

1 TOPIC	CONTEXT		QUOTE	EXPLAIN THE QUOTE	ANALYSIS
Example or Claim	WHO	TO WHOM	"You might be having some idea of ganging up on me. You could probably beat me up pretty bad. But just remember what I do to people who try to hurt me (7)."	Ender warns Stilson's friends, who could also be bullies, he will respond brutally if they ever try to harm him.	Elaboration or Rationale
Physical aggressive- ness	Ender	Stilson's friends			Like Peter, Ender is adept at using physical force. He responds quickly and is not opposed to hurting someone.
	WHEN	WHERE			
	After beating Stilson up	Near the bus stop			

2 TOPIC	CONTEXT		QUOTE	EXPLAIN THE QUOTE	ANALYSIS
Example or Claim	WHO	TO WHOM	"We had to have a commander with so much empathy that he would … understand them and anticipate them. So much compassion that he could win the love of his underlings…" (298).	Graff needed a leader who understood how the enemy was feeling and thinking, but also someone who was gentle and loving so others would follow him.	Graff knew that Ender had to be tricked or he would not have done it. Ender was kind and only forceful when he needed to be.
Compassion	Colonel Graff	Ender			
	WHEN	WHERE			
	After defeating the buggers	Ender's bedroom			

PARAGRAPH ON THE FOLLOWING PAGE (a multi-quote response)

Figure 6.10 *Ender's Game*—Sample Essay

Ender's Game
Orson Scott Card

Question: *Is Ender more like his brother Peter or his sister Valentine?*

Ender and his Siblings

Ender seems to share attributes similar to both his brother and sister, not necessarily one more than the other. Ender can be physically aggressive like Peter. When Stilson attacks Ender after school near the bus stop, Ender beats him up, kicking him until he is unconscious. Afterwards, he says to Stilson's friends, "You might be having some idea of ganging up on me. You could probably beat me up pretty bad. But just remember what I do to people who try to hurt me" (7). Ender warns Stilson's friends, who could also be bullies, he will respond brutally if they ever try to harm him. Like Peter, Ender is adept at using physical force. He responds quickly and is not opposed to hurting someone if necessary.

Ender is also like Valentine because he is also compassionate, and his leaders recognize it. After defeating the buggers and destroying their planet, Colonel Graff tells Ender in his bedroom, "We had to have a commander with so much empathy that he would ...understand them and anticipate them. So much compassion that he could win the love of his underlings . . ." (298). Graff needed a leader who understood how the enemy was feeling and thinking, but also someone who was gentle and loving so his cadets would follow him. Graff knew that Ender had to be tricked or he would not have done it. Ender was kind and only forceful when he needed to be. His gentle **nature** (like Valentine) gives him understanding, which enables his attack (like Peter) but only because he is ignorant of the real nature of his battle.

Annotations (left margin):
- Topic / Context / Quote / Explain the Quote / Analysis (first paragraph)
- Topic / Context / Quote / Explain the Quote / Analysis / Find a Link: Cause & Effect (second paragraph)

Figure 6.11 Evidence Finder 3.0—*The Watsons Go to Burningham—1963*

The Watsons Go to Birmingham—1963
Christopher Paul Curtis

I want to find evidence of <u>the shift from self-defense (or exacting justice) to bullying.</u>

1

TOPIC	CONTEXT		QUOTE	EXPLAIN THE QUOTE	ANALYSIS
Example or Claim Stolen gloves returned	WHO	TO WHOM	"[Larry Dunn] talked real tough but he didn't do a thing when Byron snatched the gloves off of his hands... That would have been fine with me but Byron wasn't through" (59).	Kenny explains how Byron forcibly took Kenny's gloves back from Larry Dunn who stole them. Byron was ready to punish the thief further.	It seems Kenny wants more than justice; he wants to humiliate Larry. Strength may stop Larry's bullying, but humiliating Larry might make it worse.
	Kenny as narrator	Reader			
	WHEN	WHERE			
	After telling Byron	By the school			

2

TOPIC	CONTEXT		QUOTE	EXPLAIN THE QUOTE	ANALYSIS
Example or Claim No concern for victim	WHO	TO WHOM	"Byron kept his word and only told me one time, then when I didn't hit Larry hard enough, By punched me in the stomach" (60).	Byron punches Kenny in the stomach for not hitting Larry.	If Byron was really concerned about Kenny as a victim, he would never have hurt Kenny for refusing to exact his version of justice.
	Kenny as narrator	Reader			
	WHEN	WHERE			
	After Byron warned him	By the school			

3

TOPIC	CONTEXT		QUOTE	EXPLAIN THE QUOTE	ANALYSIS
Example or Claim Impress the Crowd	WHO	TO WHOM	"The crowd was getting bigger and bigger and was loving this. Not because they wanted to see Larry Dunn get jacked up, but because they wanted to see anybody get it" (61).	Kenny notices how the crowd reacts to Byron mocking and beating Larry Dunn.	Byron's actions are no longer about justice; they are about humiliating the other person in front of a crowd—all for attention.
	Kenny as narrator	Reader			
	WHEN	WHERE			
	During the fight	By the school			

Figure 6.12 *The Watsons Go to Burmingham—1963*—Sample Essay

The Watsons Go to Birmingham—1963
Christopher Paul Curtis

Question: *Using Byron's fight with Larry Dunn as your focus, when does self-defense (or exacting justice) become bullying?*

From Self-Defense to Bullying

In Christopher Paul Curtis' novel <u>The Watsons Go to Birmingham—1963</u>, a boy named Larry Dunn bullies Kenny Watson until Kenny's older brother steps in to defend him. This seems appropriate, but self-defense (or defending another) can easily change into bullying itself when the purpose for fighting changes.

Topic — **Self-defense becomes revenge when the punishment is too severe. This is the case when stolen gloves are returned in the story.** **Context** — After telling his brother Byron about Larry Dunn bullying him, Kenny, who is the narrator of the story, tells the reader, **Quote** — "[Larry Dunn] talked real tough but he didn't do a thing when Byron snatched the [stolen] gloves off of his hands... That would have been fine with me but Byron wasn't through" (59). **Explain the Quote** — Kenny explains how Byron forcibly took Kenny's gloves back from Larry Dunn who stole them. But Byron was ready to punish the thief further. What was he thinking? **Analysis / Another's Point of View** — **It seems Byron wants more than justice; he wants to humiliate Larry. Byron's strength may stop Larry's bullying, but humiliating Larry might make it worse** for his younger brother. **Find a Link: Cause & Effect / If..., then... / Should- Would-Could** — **If** Byron is strong enough to stand up to Larry Dunn, **then** Byron **could have** warned him about potential consequences first, before hurting him.

Actions are no longer self-defense when the victim becomes a victim again. When the fight continues by the school, Byron wants Kenny to hit Larry while he holds him. When he hardly makes the attempt, Kenny explains, "Byron kept his word and only told me one time, then when I didn't hit Larry hard enough, By punched me in the stomach" (60). Byron punches Kenny but doesn't understand Kenny's reluctance. Unfortunately, Kenny probably

Figure 6.13 Evidence Finder 3.0—Bud, Not Buddy

EVIDENCE FINDER 3.0

Bud, Not Buddy
Christopher Paul Curtis

I want to find evidence of **the author's use of names or nicknames as symbols in the story.**

1 TOPIC	CONTEXT		QUOTE	EXPLAIN THE QUOTE	ANALYSIS
Example or Claim **Symbol of Hope**	WHO	TO WHOM	"A bud is a flower-to-be. A flower-in-waiting. Waiting for just the right warmth and care to open up. It's a little fist of love waiting to unfold and be seen by the world. And that's you" (42).	Bud's mother explains that his name comes from flower bud waiting to bloom.	Curtis' protagonist is Bud, who, like the flower, will blossom as he discovers his true identity. He must wait for the right season, or time, to bloom.
	Bud's Mom	Her son, Bud			
	WHEN	WHERE			
	A memory, after escaping	In the library			

2 TOPIC	CONTEXT		QUOTE	EXPLAIN THE QUOTE	ANALYSIS
Example or Claim **Symbol of Despair or Frustration**	WHO	TO WHOM	"'Naw, son, what you're looking for is Hooverville, with a v, like in President Herbert Hoover'… The man waved his mouth organ like a magic wand and pointed it all over the little cardboard city" (66).	Bud's host explains that Hooverville takes its name from the current president. It's a very poor place to live.	Hooverville was an actual place, but the name was intended to illustrate their irritation with the president's policies causing their suffering.
	Mouth organ man	Bud			
	WHEN	WHERE			
	Upon arriving	In Hooverville			

3 TOPIC	CONTEXT		QUOTE	EXPLAIN THE QUOTE	ANALYSIS
Example or Claim **Symbol of Unity**	WHO	TO WHOM	"On the trombone we have Chug 'Doo-Doo Bug' Cross, and the palest member of the band, on piano, is Roy 'Dirty Deed' Breed" (153).	Mr. Jimmy introduces members of their band. Each player has a unique (partly rhyming) nickname.	Nicknames represent acceptance. Even though the names are different, because every member has one, it's something they share as one.
	Mr. Jimmy	Bud			
	WHEN	WHERE			
	After introducing Steady Eddie	Onstage in the Log Cabin			

Figure 6.14 *Bud, Not Buddy*—Sample Essay

Bud, Not Buddy
Christopher Paul Curtis

Question: *How does the author use names (or nicknames) as symbols?*

Names as Symbols

In his novel <u>Bud, not Buddy</u>, author Christopher Paul Curtis uses names (or nicknames) as symbols to represent different aspects of characters and ideas in the story. **Names are very important in this story, and the lead character, Bud, is one who has a name for a specific purpose. His name is a symbol of his mother's love and hope for his life.** In the story, after Bud escapes an orphanage and finds a place to hide in a library, he remembers something his mother told him about his name: "A bud is a flower-to-be. A flower-in-waiting. Waiting for just the right warmth and care to open up. It's a little fist of love waiting to unfold and be seen by the world. And that's you" (42). Bud's mother explains that his name comes from flower bud waiting to bloom. Bud, who, **like the flower, will blossom** as he discovers his true identity. He must wait for the right season, or time, to bloom. His mother could see his potential, and she wanted him to see it, too.

In addition to representing hope, Curtis also uses names to signify other feelings like despair and frustration. One nickname he uses describes a place, not a person: Hooverville. Upon arriving in the shanty town, a man who played the mouth organ says to Bud, "'Naw, son, what you're looking for is Hooverville, with a v, like in President Herbert Hoover'…The man waved his mouth organ like a magic wand and pointed it all over the little cardboard city" (66). Hooverville was an actual place, but the name was intended to illustrate their irritation with the president's policies causing their suffering. The town's name symbolizes their disgust.

Labels (left margin):
- Topic
- Context
- Quote
- Explain the Quote / Analysis
- Says This, Means That

Figure 6.15 Evidence Finder 3.0—Holes

EVIDENCE FINDER 3.0

Holes
Louis Sachar

I want to find evidence of how the author uses conventions to enhance his story.

1	TOPIC	CONTEXT		QUOTE	EXPLAIN THE QUOTE	ANALYSIS
Example or Claim		WHO	TO WHOM	"Whenever anything went wrong, they always blamed Stanley's no-good-dirty-rotten-pig-stealing-great-great grandfather" (7).	Sachar uses hyphens to create a new epithet for his grandfather, not a very nice one.	Because of the hyphen, an ordinary character becomes extraordinary. His kin is now infamous and much more memorable for the reader.
	Hyphen	Louis Sachar	Reader			
		WHEN	WHERE			
		While riding	On the bus to Camp Green			

2	TOPIC	CONTEXT		QUOTE	EXPLAIN THE QUOTE	ANALYSIS
Example or Claim		WHO	TO WHOM	"While the wolf waits below, hungry and lonely, / He cries to the mo—oo—oon, 'If only, if only'" (8).	Stanley enjoys the memory. Every time his father would sing the word "moon," he would howl it like a wolf might sing it.	Sachar uses a dash to represent a funny pronunciation. It creates an image of a loving father pretending to be a wolf.
	Dash	Memory of Father	Stanley			
		WHEN	WHERE			
		While riding	On the bus to Camp Green			

3	TOPIC	CONTEXT		QUOTE	EXPLAIN THE QUOTE	ANALYSIS
Example or Claim		WHO	TO WHOM	"Everyone in his family had always liked the fact that 'Stanley Yelnats' was spelled the same frontward and backward" (9).	Sachar uses Stanley's name like a mirror, which technique is a palindrome.	Spelling his name this way makes it more memorable. Sachar might want Stanley to see hope when all he sees is bad luck.
	Spelling	Author	Reader			
		WHEN	WHERE			
		Introducing family	In the exposition			

Figure 6.16 *Holes*—Sample Essay

Holes
Louis Sachar

Question: *How does the author use conventions to enhance his story?*

Names as Symbols

What are conventions? They are writing tools like punctuation marks and correct spelling. Louis Sachar, author of the young adult novel Holes uses conventions to enhance his story in different ways.

Topic — **One punctuation mark Sachar uses is a hyphen.** In the
Context — story, while his character Stanley rides on a bus to Camp Green Lake, the author tells the reader, "Whenever anything went
Quote — wrong, they always blamed Stanley's no-good-dirty-rotten-pig-stealing-great-great grandfather" (7). Sachar uses hyphens to
Explain the Quote — create an epithet for his grandfather, not a very nice one.
Analysis — However, because of the hyphen, an **ordinary person becomes extraordinary.** Stanley's kin is now infamous, making him more
Find a link: Cause & Effect — memorable for the reader. **If** Sachar **would** have written
If..., Then... — "grandfather" by itself, **then** the character would not have been as interesting.

Sachar uses another punctuation mark to develop his story—a dash. Still on the bus to Camp Green Lake, Stanley remembers his father singing to him: "While the wolf waits below, hungry and lonely, / He cries to the mo—oo—oon, 'If only, if only'" (8). Stanley enjoys the memory. Every time his father would sing the word "moon," he would howl it like a wolf might sing it. Sachar uses a dash to represent a funny pronunciation. It creates an image of a loving father pretending to be a wolf.

And finally, Sachar uses creative spelling to introduce his protagonist, Stanley Yelnats. In the exposition portion of the book, the author tells the reader, "Everyone in his family had

Figure 6.17 Evidence Finder 1.0—*Tuck Everlasting*

EVIDENCE FINDER 1.0

Tuck Everlasting
Natalie Babbitt

I want to find evidence of Winnie making a wise (or unwise) decision in refusing to drink water that would make her immortal.

3	TOPIC	CONTEXT		QUOTE	EXPLAIN THE QUOTE	ANALYSIS
	Real Family	WHO	TO WHOM	"In Loving Memory / Winifred Foster Jackson / Dear Wife / Dear Mother / 1870-1948. (138)"	The inscription explains that Winnie was remembered lovingly by her husband and children. She lived seventy-eight years.	Clearly Winnie had an opportunity to find love because her family took the time to create a monument for her.
		Author (epitaph)	Reader (Tuck reads)			
		WHEN	WHERE			
		Two years after Winnie	At the cemetery in Treegap			

Topic — **Winnie made the correct decision to refuse the drink of water that would make her immortal because she was able to experience a very special life with a real family.** Tuck travels to Treegap to find Winnie, but it is too late. She

Context — has already died. He finds her epitaph that reads: "In Loving Memory /

Quote — Winifred Foster Jackson / Dear Wife / Dear Mother / 1870 -1948" (138). The

Explain the Quote — inscription explains that Winnie was remembered lovingly by her husband and children. She lived seventy-eight years. **Clearly** Winnie had an opportunity to

Analysis — find love **because** her family took the time to create a monument for her. She

Another's Point of View — **may** not have lived forever, but when she lived, she experienced real joy. Winnie probably wondered if she **could** live a life without being truly close to a

Should-Would-Could — family of her own. To her, it just wasn't worth it. If I were Winnie's child, I wouldn't want her to live forever without me.

Figure 6.18 Evidence Finder 3.0—*Star Girl*

EVIDENCE FINDER 3.0

Stargirl
Jerry Spinelli

I want to find evidence of how Stargirl is different from other teenagers.

1 TOPIC	CONTEXT		QUOTE	EXPLAIN THE QUOTE	ANALYSIS
Example or Claim: Notices details about others' lives	WHO: Narrator	TO WHOM: Reader	"The five-column photo in the Times showed Danny on his father's shoulders, surrounded by a mob of neighbors. Danny's safe. In the foreground was a new bike, and big sign that read: WELCOME HOME DANNY."	The author details how many loved ones celebrated Danny's safe return home. A new bike was waiting for him.	If Stargirl was the one who left the bike (and it seems she was), then she is different because she purchased an expensive gift for a stranger.
	WHEN: After Danny Pike's accident	WHERE: Mica Times newspaper			

2 TOPIC	CONTEXT		QUOTE	EXPLAIN THE QUOTE	ANALYSIS
Example or Claim: Celebrates everyone's success	WHO: Author	TO WHOM: Audience	"And right there in the middle of it all, in the midst of this perfect season mania, was Stargirl, popping up whenever the ball went through the net, no matter which team scored...."	Apparently, Stargirl cheers for both teams when they make a basket during the game.	Most young people do not cheer for others' success during a competitive game. Stargirl wants both sides to do well, not just her own team.
	WHEN: During a January game	WHERE: In the stands			

3 TOPIC	CONTEXT		QUOTE	EXPLAIN THE QUOTE	ANALYSIS
Example or Claim: Changes Own Name	WHO: Stargirl	TO WHOM: Kevin	"I'm not my name. My name is something I wear, like a shirt. It gets worn out, I outgrow it, I change it."	Stargirl uses a simile to compare her name to clothing, something that gets used and then discarded.	Stargirl knows that a name is just a name. She uses it; it does not use her. It may be different, but she has the right to change it if it no longer fits.
	WHEN: Responding to his question	WHERE: At the studio			

Figure 6.19 *Star Girl*—Sample Essay

Stargirl
Jerry Spinelli

Question: *How is Stargirl different from normal teenagers? Is it wise for her to be this way?*

The Courage to Be Different

In author Jerry Spinelli's novel <u>Stargirl</u>, a young woman with the same name is different than typical teenagers. These differences cause her unnecessary ridicule, which makes her decisions appear unwise, but her life is one that makes her happy—and maybe others, too.

One way Stargirl is different is in the way she seems to notice the details of other people's lives. For example, the narrator tells the reader that a young nine-year-old boy named Danny Pike wrecked on his bicycle, causing complications that threatened his life. When he finally returns home safely, the author explains what was written in the <u>Mica Times</u> newspaper: "The five-column photo in the *Times* showed Danny on his father's shoulders, surrounded by a mob of neighbors. In the foreground was a new bike, and big sign that read: WELCOME HOME DANNY." The author details how many loved ones celebrated Danny's safe return home. A new bike was waiting for him. **If** Stargirl was the one who left the bike (and it seems she was), **then** she is different because she purchased an expensive gift for a stranger. Others may have known about Danny's accident, but she was the only one who provided a gift. And it was a secret. Other teens give, but Stargirl gives without caring if others know. She **could have** admitted her gift, but she didn't.

Stargirl is more than giving; she also celebrates the success of others, even when it doesn't follow tradition. During a January basketball game, Stargirl cheers in the stands. The author writes, "And right there in the middle of it all, in the midst of this perfect season mania, was Stargirl, popping up whenever

Annotations (left margin, with arrows pointing into the essay):
- **Topic**
- **Context**
- **Quote**
- **Explain the Quote**
- **Analysis** *If..., then...*
- **Should-Would-Could**

Figure 6.20 Evidence Finder 2.1—*The Adventures of Tom Sawyer*

EVIDENCE FINDER 2.1

The Adventures of Tom Sawyer
Mark Twain

I want to find evidence of <u>how boys want something more if they are told they can't have it.</u>

From the text

1	TOPIC	CONTEXT		QUOTE	EXPLAIN THE QUOTE	ANALYSIS
	EXAMPLE or CLAIM	WHO	TO WHOM	"No—no—I reckon it wouldn't hardly do . . . I reckon there ain't one boy in a thousand, maybe two thousand, that can do it the way it's got to be done."	Tom denies Ben's request to attempt painting the fence. He tells his friend that few boys could get it right.	ELABORATE
	Whitewashing the fence	Tom	His friend Ben			It appears the more Tom withholds a chance, the more Ben wants to do his work.
		WHEN	WHERE			
		After Ben asks to try	In Aunt Polly's front yard			

From my own life

2	TOPIC	CONTEXT		PERSONAL EXPERIENCE	CONNECTION
	EVENT	WHO WAS THERE		For a long time I would pull weeds or cut them with a shovel while my dad would push the lawn mower in our backyard. He told me that pushing a lawn mower was for "older boys" and didn't want me to get hurt. When I asked if I could try, he told me I would have to wait till I was "strong enough." I told him I was! After that, I mowed every week by myself.	Like Ben, I would have given my apple to try. Now I realize what I learned: When my dad said no, it made me want to try even more.
	Lawn mower	My dad and I			
		WHEN	WHERE		
		When I was nine	In my backyard		

Figure 6.21 *The Adventures of Tom Sawyer*—Sample Essay

The Adventures of Tom Sawyer
Mark Twain

Question: Twain writes in Chapter 2: "In order to make a man or a boy covet a thing, it is only necessary to make the thing difficult to attain." How might this have been true for Tom? Is this true for you?

Denial Creates Desire

In his novel <u>The Adventures of Tom Sawyer</u>, Mark Twain writes: "In order to make a man or a boy covet a thing, it is only necessary to make the thing difficult to attain." This was true for Tom (the title character), and it is true for me, also.

Boys always seem to want something they can't have. For example, in the story, Tom has to work on a Saturday whitewashing a fence as a punishment. While Tom is painting Aunt Polly's front yard fence, Ben asks to try. Tom tells his friend, "No—no—I reckon it wouldn't hardly do. . .I reckon there ain't one boy in a thousand, maybe two thousand, that can do it the way it's got to be done." Tom denies Ben's request to attempt painting the fence. He tells his friend that few boys could get it right. **It appears** the more Tom withholds a chance, the more Ben wants to do his work.

I experienced something similar working with my dad while learning to use a lawnmower. He and I have worked in the backyard since I was nine years old. For a long time I would pull weeds or cut them with a shovel while my dad would push the lawn mower in our backyard. He told me that pushing a lawn mower was for "older boys" and didn't want me to get hurt. When I asked if I could try, he told me I would have to wait till I was "strong enough." I told him I was! After that, I mowed every week by myself. **Like Ben, I would have given my apple for an opportunity. Now I realize what I learned: When my dad said no, it made me want to try even more. If Tom would have** let the boy try right when he first asked, it is likely he would not have wanted to do Tom's work for him as badly.

Labels (left margin): Topic, Context, Quote, Explain the Quote, Analysis, Topic, Context, Personal Experience, Connection, If..., then..., Should-Would-Could

Figure 6.22 Evidence Finder 3.0—*The Declaration of Independence*

EVIDENCE FINDER 3.0

The Declaration of Independence
Thomas Jefferson

I want to find evidence of <u>how the organization might have impacted King George's reaction.</u>

1 TOPIC	\multicolumn{2}{c}{CONTEXT}	QUOTE	EXPLAIN THE QUOTE	ANALYSIS
Example or Claim	WHO	TO WHOM	"It becomes necessary for one people to dissolve the political bands… and to assume among the powers of the requires that they should declare the causes which impel them to the separation."	Jefferson asserts that sometimes nations have a right to declare and provide reasons for their independence.	King George would likely have been very angry to read an introduction from his former subjects declaring they were equal.
Preamble	Jefferson	King George			
	WHEN	WHERE			
	To begin	His declaration			

2 TOPIC	CONTEXT		QUOTE	EXPLAIN THE QUOTE	ANALYSIS
Example or Claim	WHO	TO WHOM	"Governments are instituted among Men, deriving their just powers from the consent of the governed."	Jefferson affirms that a government's creation and power comes from the voice of those who are governed.	The next section would have further angered him because it openly declares that democracy gives power, not a royal title.
Self-Evident Truths	Jefferson	King George and world			
	WHEN	WHERE			
	After the preamble	In the second section			

3 TOPIC	CONTEXT		QUOTE	EXPLAIN THE QUOTE	ANALYSIS
Example or Claim	WHO	TO WHOM	"He has plundered our seas, ravaged our coasts, burnt our towns, and destroyed the loves of our people.…"	In the center portion of the declaration, Jefferson describes in list form some of the many abuses King George caused colonists to suffer.	The king may have interpreted these actions differently, believing he had the right and power to control his subjects.
Grievances	Jefferson	King George			
	WHEN	WHERE			
	After self-evident truths	In the third section			

Figure 6.23 *The Declaration of Independence*—Sample Essay

The Declaration of Independence
Thomas Jefferson

Question: *How might Jefferson's organization of* The Declaration of Independence *have affected King George's reaction?*

Order and Power

In his foundational document <u>The Declaration of Independence</u>, Thomas Jefferson represented a new nation. How he organized his document emphasized his content and probably affected his audience's—King George's—reaction.

[Topic] **Jefferson first chooses to introduce his treatise with a preamble that justifies when it is appropriate for a nation to declare independence.** [Context] To begin his declaration to King George, Jefferson writes: [Quote] "It becomes necessary for one people to dissolve the political bands …and to assume among the powers of the earth, the separate and equal station…[and] requires that they should declare the causes which impel them to the separation." [Explain the Quote] Jefferson asserts that sometimes nations have a right to declare and provide reasons for their independence. [Analysis] King George **would likely have been** very angry to read an introduction from his former subjects declaring they were equal. [Another's Point of View] By beginning with such a bold preface, Jefferson would likely have **caused** King George **to immediately want revenge** militarily. But it also **probably caused** the king to read further. [Cause and Effect] Jefferson could have started with his **grievances first**, but starting this way gives the document strength because it is based on a core truth, even beyond their own conflict. Only **after this** foundation would it make sense to provide principles. [Ranking]

These principles make up self-evident truths that would surely have made King George angry. In the second section, following the preamble, Jefferson speaks to King George but potentially all people when he says, "Governments are instituted among Men, deriving their just powers from the consent of the governed."

Figure 6.24 Evidence Finder 1.0—*Letter from Birmingham Jail*

Letter from Birmingham Jail
Martin Luther King, Jr.

I want to find evidence of <u>how King felt about creating tension in a community.</u>

1	TOPIC	CONTEXT		QUOTE	EXPLAIN THE QUOTE	ANALYSIS
	Tension in a community	WHO	TO WHOM	"I have worked and preached against violent tension, but there is a type of constructive nonviolent tension that is necessary for growth."	By "growth," King meant racial equality. King believed that creating nonviolent friction was necessary for actual changes to occur.	Creating change is more effective when people feel a sense of urgency or discomfort. When I suffer, I want my situation to change. Opposition can help.
		Martin Luther King, Jr.	White religious leaders			
		WHEN	WHERE			
		April 16, 1963	Jail, Birmingham, Alabama			

Topic ⟶ **Tension is a state of uneasiness, where not everything fits together or where people may feel discomfort because they disagree. Civil rights leader Martin Luther King, Jr., believed that tension was necessary in his community to invite real change, and I agree with him.** While in jail in Birmingham, Alabama,

Context ⟶ in 1963, King wrote to white religious leaders who publicly expressed concern over his methods. He responded in his public letter, "I have worked and

Quote ⟶ preached against violent tension, but there is a type of constructive nonviolent tension that is necessary for growth." By "growth," King meant racial equality.

Explain the Quote ⟶ He believed that creating nonviolent friction was necessary for actual changes to occur. He didn't want people to be hurt, but he also doesn't want people to feel comfortable with so many suffering from racial injustice. Creating change

Analysis ⟶ is more effective when people feel a sense of urgency or discomfort. When I suffer, I know I want things to change. Opposition helps me learn and grow.

130 ◆ Extra Examples Using Mentor Texts

Figure 6.25 Evidence Finder 3.0—*The Star Spangled Banner*

EVIDENCE FINDER 3.0

The Star Spangled Banner
Francis Scott Key

I want to find evidence of important colonial beliefs found in the Star Spangled Banner.

1 TOPIC	CONTEXT		QUOTE	EXPLAIN THE QUOTE	ANALYSIS
Example or Claim: Value of Bravery	WHO: Key	TO WHOM: Fellow Americans (Ft. McHenry)	"[…] Whose broad stripes and bright stars through the perilous fight / O'er the ramparts we watched, were so gallantly streaming? …O'er the land of the free and the home of the brave."	Key describes seeing the stars and stripes still positioned above the ramparts, or fortifications the British had, been bombing.	The flag becomes a symbol of bravery when times are "perilous". Americans today also respect courage, defending our country from threats.
	WHEN: When introducing the banner	WHERE: 1st Verse / and Refrain			

2 TOPIC	CONTEXT		QUOTE	EXPLAIN THE QUOTE	ANALYSIS
Example or Claim: Slavery and Freedom	WHO: Key	TO WHOM: Audience	"No refuge could save the hireling and slave/ From the terror of flight, or the gloom of the grave."	Slaves and freemen alike could not escape the fear common when fleeing or dying in battle.	Ironically, Americans recognized slavery at the same time they believed in freedom. We no longer believe in slavery; we respect the rights of all.
	WHEN: After asking where British	WHERE: In the 3rd verse			

3 TOPIC	CONTEXT		QUOTE	EXPLAIN THE QUOTE	ANALYSIS
Example or Claim: Trusting in God	WHO: Key	TO WHOM: Readers	"Blest with vict'ry and peace, may the Heaven' rescued land / Praise the Power that hat made and preserved us a nation / Then conquer we must, when our cause it is just,/ And this be our motto: 'In God is our trust.'"	Key posits that divine Power (with a capital), or God, blessed and "preserved" them during battle.	Early Americans must have felt a deep respect for trusting in God's help. I think Americans generally believe in God, though some do not.
	WHEN: Upon concluding	WHERE: His final verse			

Figure 6.26 *The Star Spangled Banner*—Sample Essay

The Star Spangled Banner
Francis Scott Key

Question(s): *How do lyrics from* The Star Spangled Banner *(Francis Scott Key's poem "The Defence of Fort McHenry") reflect early American values? Are those values shared today?*

Topic	**Key to American Beliefs**
	Francis Scott Key wrote a poem called "The Defence of Fort McHenry," which later became *The Star Spangled Banner*, America's national anthem. Key's lyrics reflect early-American beliefs that are generally valued today, also.
Context	**One such value of early Americans was bravery, standing up against tyranny and danger.** When introducing the banner in the first verse (or stanza), Key seems to relate his experience at Fort Henry, telling his fellow Americans of the flag "whose
Quote	broad stripes and bright stars through the perilous fight / O'er the ramparts we watched, were so gallantly streaming ... O'er the land of the free and the home of the brave." Key
Explain the Quote	describes seeing the stars and stripes still positioned above the ramparts, or fortifications, the British had been bombing.
Analysis	The flag becomes a **symbol** of bravery when times are "perilous".
Says This, Means That	Americans today also respect courage, defending our country from threats like terrorism. When Americans or our soldiers are scared, we **could** give up or ignore the problem. We **could**
Should-Would-Could	let others suffer around the world and disregard their needs, but this **would** leave others fearful. By **being brave,** we **help**
Cause and Effect	**others be valiant** when challenges arise.
	Early Americans also supported freedom—and (some) slavery. After asking where the British threat were hiding, in his third verse Key writes, "No refuge could save the hireling and slave / From the terror of flight, or the gloom of the grave." Slaves and freemen alike could not escape the fear common when fleeing or dying in battle. Ironically, Americans abhorred tyranny but embraced slavery.

Figure 6.27 Evidence Finder 3.0—*The Ransom of Red Chief*

EVIDENCE FINDER 3.0

The Ransom of Red Chief
O. Henry

I want to find evidence of how O. Henry uses irony to enhance his story, the "Ransom of Red Chief."

1 TOPIC	CONTEXT		QUOTE	EXPLAIN THE QUOTE	ANALYSIS
Example or Claim	WHO	TO WHOM	"There was a town down there, as flat as a flannel-cake, and called Summit, of course."	Sam sets the scene for the story in a flat town named after a mountain or summit.	O. Henry seems to foreshadow the irony that will be found in the whole story when the very location of it is something different than it appears.
To Establish Setting	Sam as Narrator	Reader			
	WHEN	WHERE			
	To begin his story	In the exposition			

2 TOPIC	CONTEXT		QUOTE	EXPLAIN THE QUOTE	ANALYSIS
Example or Claim	WHO	TO WHOM	"Philoprogenitiveness, says we, is strong in semi-rural communities; therefore and for other reasons, a kidnapping project ought to do better there than… to stir up talk about such things."	Sam and Bill decide that "philoprogenitiveness" or love for offspring is strong in Summit, giving them more reason to kidnap Red Chief.	Sam and Bill use such strong diction that it becomes ironic: their words make them appear intelligent, but they are easily abused by Red Chief, a boy.
To Build Characters	Sam, adding friend Bill	Audience			
	WHEN	WHERE			
	While forming a plan	Front steps of hotel			

3 TOPIC	CONTEXT		QUOTE	EXPLAIN THE QUOTE	ANALYSIS
Example or Claim	WHO	TO WHOM	"I think you are a little high in your demands, and I here by make you a counter- proposition…. You bring Johnny home and pay me two hundred and fifty dollars in cash and I agree to take him off your hands."	Dorsett proposes a counter-offer, saying he will only take his son back if they pay him $250 dollars.	O. Henry uses irony in a final plot twist: Sam and Bill are happy with paying money to return Red Chief, whom they kidnapped.
To Develop Plot	Ebenezer Dorsett, boy's father	Sam and Bill			
	WHEN	WHERE			
	After the ransom request	In his response to the ransom			

Extra Examples Using Mentor Texts ◆ 133

Figure 6.28 *The Ransom of Red Chief*—Sample Essay

The Ransom of Red Chief
O. Henry

Question: How does O. Henry's use irony to develop his story, "The Ransom of Red Chief"?

O Irony

In his story "The Ransom of Red Chief," author O. Henry uses irony to develop his setting, characters, and plot. **Henry uses irony to introduce his setting.** To begin his story Sam, speaking as the narrator, tells the reader as part of his exposition, "There was a town down there, as flat as a flannel-cake, and called Summit, of course." Sam sets the scene for the story in a flat town named after a mountain or summit, completely opposite. O. Henry **seems to foreshadow** the irony that will be found in the whole story when the very location of it is something different than it appears. The irony **causes** the reader to anticipate other possible contradictions. The irony **creates** humor for the reader.

After using irony to establish the location of the story, Henry continues using irony, this time to build his characters. While forming a plan on the front steps of the hotel, Sam (adding his friend Bill Driscoll) tells the audience, "Philoprogenitiveness, says we, is strong in semi-rural communities; therefore and for other reasons, a kidnapping project ought to do better there than… to stir up talk about such things." Sam and Bill decide that "philoprogenitiveness" or love for offspring is strong in Summit, giving them more reason to kidnap Red Chief. Sam and Bill use such strong diction that it becomes ironic: their words make them appear intelligent, but they are easily abused by Red Chief, a boy. We expect them to be successful because of their confident words, but this is not the case.

Annotations (left margin):
- Topic
- Context
- Quote
- Explain the Quote
- Analysis
- Cause and Effect

Figure 6.29 Evidence Finder 3.0—*Inaugural Address, 1961*

EVIDENCE FINDER 3.0

Inaugural Address, 1961
John F. Kennedy

I want to find evidence of Kennedy proposing a solution to the national fear of the atomic bomb.

1	TOPIC	CONTEXT		QUOTE	EXPLAIN THE QUOTE	ANALYSIS
Example or Claim	Peaceful negotiation	WHO	TO WHOM	"So let us begin anew—remembering on both sides that civility is not a sign of weakness, and sincerity is always subject to proof. Let us never negotiate out of fear. But let us never fear to negotiate."	Kennedy reminds potential enemies that negotiation is a sign of strength, not weakness.	I agree with Kennedy's assertion. By saying these words, he enables world leaders to talk without feeling like they should be embarrassed for negotiating.
		Kennedy	America's adversaries			
		WHEN	WHERE			
		After calling for defense	Inaugural address			

Topic — **One of Kennedy's proposed solutions to the national fear of the atomic bomb is to invite other countries to participate in peaceful negotiation.** In his inaugural

Context — address, after calling for a strong defense so that others will not be tempted to fight

Quote — us, Kennedy addresses America's potential adversaries, saying, "So let us begin anew—remember on both sides that civility is not a sign of weakness, and sincerity is always subject to proof. Let us never negotiate out of fear. But let us never fear to

Explain the Quote — negotiate." Kennedy reminds potential enemies that negotiation is a sign of strength,

Analysis — not weakness. **I agree** with Kennedy's assertion. By saying these words, he enables

Agree / Disagree — world leaders to talk without feeling like they should be embarrassed for negotiating.

Another's Point of View — **If other countries feel** intimidated by the US, they **may** have a hard time trusting an opportunity to work through differences. **When I look through other world leaders'**

Cause and Effect — **eyes**, I realize they have a large group of people to consider. Kennedy's invitation could open the door for meaningful conversation.

7

Bonus Tool: Cue Cards to Teach Literary Terms

To *analyze* a text—that is, to identify and label its parts—you may first want students to know definitions of literary devices (*knowledge*) and be able to explain their use (*comprehension*). But how do we make such terms easy to understand and hard to forget?

I recommend using "cue cards." These giant flash cards can be placed around your classroom for students to refer to at all times. Each laminated (homemade) sign in my classroom is about 15" x 20", big enough to see from around the room. Cutting a poster board into four equal pieces works well. Simply choose the terms that best suit your grade level and place cards on walls for students to see. Each box features a mnemonic—a picture, a rhyme, a symbol, a sentence starter—anything to help students remember an **anchor definition** for regular reference. Freely substitute your own mnemonic, if desired. As you might expect, simple definitions can sometimes cloud actual usage (or even neglect an additional definition). However, a teacher's explanation usually solves the problem. I will be the first to recognize the imperfect nature of these cards but find them valuable nonetheless. Mnemonics help students retain the *gist*, while teachers' reiteration clarifies the *nuance*. Gradually, students no longer need the mnemonic to recite definitions or find examples.

Literary Terms Packet

Miniature versions like those on the following pages allow for separate lessons, or a literary-terms packet, or computer-projected visual for students. I thought of placing terms alphabetically for faster reference, but the practicality of having similar terms on a *pull-and-use* page seems more user-friendly when teaching a unit from general to specific. The challenge: As terms vary widely and often overlap genres, it remains unrealistic to organize them perfectly. Still, general groupings are possible: **figurative language** terms comprise numbers 1–15; **story** terms 16–37; **poetry** terms 38–56; and **miscellaneous** 57–75. Students could mark the tiny corner boxes when terms are assigned or mastered.

Sometimes I ask my class to write brief definitions, answers, or other notations in each term's box while I teach the term; alternatively, I may use the packet as an assessment tool following a unit where I used the *wall-approach* to introduce and practice terms. Either way (or both), chunking information has proven very effective. Students can use them as flash cards quizzing each other.

Viraling

One fun way to invite mastery is to use a technique I call "viraling." I take one student around the room quizzing that person on all the cue cards. If that person gets them all right, then he or she is "approved"; in other words, that person is now a teacher like me and can select another student to take around the room. Each time a new student completes the list perfectly, the process continues and before too long, students are at various places around the room quizzing each other over definitions. The process soon spreads like a virus, hence the term *viraling*. It's fun because it gets students out of their desks for a few minutes. It also holds students accountable for knowing all the terms, and it allows me to check for understanding by yoking the strength of my entire class. Students seem to take the responsibility very seriously, prompting and filling in the gaps when their peers need extra nurturing.

Following a key, a single poem and (fictional) story are included for close reading demonstration and practice. Not all terms are represented, but perhaps you will get ideas for exercises or assessments.

Figure 7.1 Figurative Language Cue Cards

| A | **Figurative Language** | Name: _____ |

| 1 **Figurative Language** Says one thing, _____ | 2 **Simile** Comparison using _____ or _____ | 3 **Metaphor** ___ is ___ ___ are ___ ___ of ___ |

| 4 **Personification** The <u>moon smiled</u> down on us. | 5 **Hyperbole** "I've told you a <u>million</u> times…" (Extreme Ex-_____) | 6 **Understatement** "It's a bit breezy outside." |

| 7 **Symbol** = LOVE | 8 **Cliché (or Idiom)** "Think outside the box." | 9 **Connotation** _____ definition |

| 10 **Denotation** _____ definition (not figurative) | 11 **Pun** 1 Expression with 2 _____ | 12 **Euphemism** "Passed away" Vs. Died |

| 13 **Epithet** King of Rock 'n Roll | 14 **Verbal Irony** When someone says one thing, but…. | 15 **Synecdoche** "Bring your wheels around to the front of the school." |

Figure 7.2 Story Cue Cards

B **Story** Name: _____

16 Theme

The main _____

17 Motif

A mini- _____

18 Plot Diagram

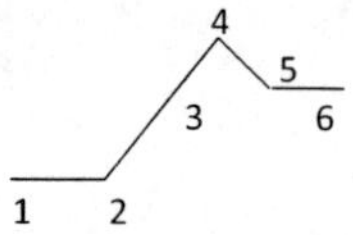

19 Exposition

Introduce

_____ & _____

20 Conflict

What goes _____

21 Rising Action

S _____
P _____
S _____
P _____

22 Climax

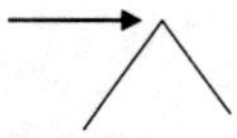

Highest _____ in a _____
OR Most critical _____

23-24 Falling Action

What happens after the _____

Resolution

Problem solved or...

L _____ L _____

25 Characterization

To develop a character using:

26-30 Conflict Types: Man vs. ___

31 Archetype

The Wiseman...
The Fool...
The Hero...

32 Dialogue

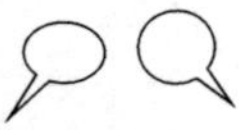

33-35 Point of View

1st Person _____
2nd Person _____
3rd Person _____
 Objective
 Limited
 Omniscient

36 Foreshadowing

H _ _ _

37 Show, Don't Tell

She was sad. = **Tell**

Vs.

_____ = Show

Figure 7.3 Poetry Cue Cards

| C | Poetry | Name: _____ |

38-39
Prose

_____ writing

Poetry

_____ writing

40
Verse

1
↘ _____

Of poetry or scripture

41
Stanza

~~~~~~~~~
~~~~~~~~~
~~~~~~~~~
~~~~~~~~~

42-45
Couplet ___

Tercet ___

Quatrain ___

Cinquain ___

46
Refrain

Repeated _____

(In music it's called a _____.)

47
Rhyme Scheme

~~~~~~~~~~A
~~~~~~~~~~B
~~~~~~~~~~A
~~~~~~~~~~B

48
End Rhyme

Rhymes at the ____

49
Internal Rhyme

Rhymes in the ____

50
Near Rhyme

Almost _____

51
Free Verse

No _____

52
Foot

Pattern (or footprint) of stressed and unstressed
S_____

(Clap: It creates the rhythm.)

53
Meter

Repeat the _____

54
Alliteration

Mickey Mouse

55
Consonance

My ankle broke and ached all day.

56
Assonance

I believe what the teacher sees in me.

Figure 7.4 Miscellaneous Cue Cards

D

Miscellaneous

Name: _____

---

57 Infer

_____
READ

---

58 Imagery

Picture with _____

59-60

Tone = ✏️

Vs.

Mood = 👓

---

61 Anecdote

Short (true) _____

---

62 Fable

Story with a _____
often using _____

---

63 Satire

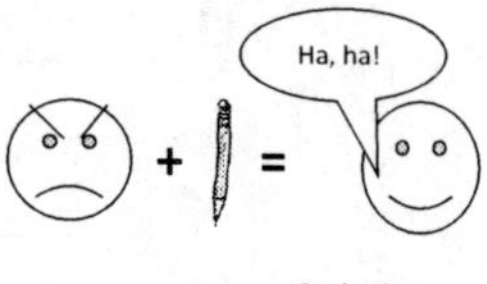

😠 + ✏️ = 😊 "Ha, ha!"

Goal: Change

---

64 Legend

Story from PAST that cannot be _____.

---

65 Myth

🌍

---

66 Folktale

○—— Story Baton

---

67 Situational Irony

When you expect one thing to happen, but _____

---

68 Onomatopoeia

Buzz!
Pop!
Splash!
Crackle!

---

69 Pseudonym

AKA

---

70 Allusion

Reference to _____

71-72 Syntax

_____ Fluency

Diction

_____ Choice

73-75 Parallelism

BONUS:
Anaphora   Epistrophe
~~~~~   ~~~~~
^^^^^   ^^^^^

Figure 7.5 Literary Terms Packet Key

Figurative Language

1. **Figurative Language**: NOT literal (Says one thing, means another)
2. **Simile**: Comparison using like or as
3. **Metaphor**: Comparison (generally) using *is*, *are*, or *of*. ("Was" and "were" also work.)
   Examples: Our relationship **is** a **storm**. Men **are** dogs. We had a war of words.
4. **Personification**: Giving a non-human thing human-like characteristics
5. **Hyperbole**: Extreme Exaggeration; to over-exaggerate
6. **Understatement:** To under-exaggerate
7. **Symbol**: Something that represents something else (usually a person, place, or thing representing an idea); e.g., a flower representing love
8. **Cliché or Idiom**: Over-used (common) expression
9. **Connotation:** slang (implied or nuanced) definition;
10. **Denotation:** literal or dictionary definition (not figurative language)
11. **Pun**: 1 expression with 2 meanings
12. **Euphemism**: Softer way of saying something difficult
13. **Epithet:** Nickname or Term of Endearment
    Example: King of Rock 'n Roll = Elvis Presley
14. **Verbal Irony:** When someone says one thing, but the opposite is true while saying it.
    Example: It's clear as mud. OR: There will be no name calling, idiot!
15. **Synecdoche:** Referring to the part, meaning the whole (*wheels* for car or *heart* for self)
    Example: Bring your *wheels* around to the front of the school. **OR** I gave him my *heart*.

Story

B

16. **Theme:** The main idea
17. **Motif:** A mini-theme; something that repeats (words, actions, objects) in a story
18. **Plot Diagram:**   1 = Exposition, 2 = Conflict, 3 = Rising Action,
                         4 = Climax, 5 = Falling Action, 6 = Denouement
19. **Exposition:** Introduce Setting & Characters
20. **Conflict:** What goes wrong; see also *Conflict Types: Man vs.* ___
21. **Rising Action:** Intensity increases through problem, solution, problem, solution, etc.
22. **Climax:** Highest point in a story **OR** Most critical decision.
23. **Falling Action**: What happens after the climax
24. **Resolution**: Biggest problem solved; Lesson Learned
25. **Characterization:** To develop a character using thoughts, words, and actions.
26-30. **Conflict Types: Man vs.** ___ : Man, Self (smiley face), Society, Nature, Supernatural
31. **Archetype:** Typical characters in stories around the world
32. **Dialogue:** Two or more people talking
33. **1st Person Point of View:**   I ; (I went to the store.)
34. **2nd Person Point of View:**   you ; (Do you want to go to the store?)
35. **3rd Person Point of View:** he, she, they; (She went to the store.)
    Objective: Narrator not in the story; **Limited**: Told from one character's point of view
    Omniscient: All-seeing (through multiple characters' eyes; their thoughts)
36. **Foreshadowing:** HINT of what will happen
37. **Show, Don't Tell:** *She was sad.* = Tell Vs. *She began to cry.* = Show

Figure 7.5 Continued

C

Poetry

38. **Prose:** Paragraph (or sentence) writing
39. **Poetry:** Artful (or stanzaic) writing
40. **Verse:** 1 <u>Line</u> of poetry or scripture
41. **Stanza:** Basic unit of poetry
42. **Couplet:** 2-line stanza
43. **Tercet:** 3-line stanza
44. **Quatrain**: 4-line stanza
45. **Cinquain:** 5-line stanza
46. **Refrain:** repeated stanza; in a song it's called a *chorus*
47. **Rhyme Scheme:** pattern of rhyme in a stanza
48. **End Rhyme:** rhyme at the end
49. **Internal Rhyme:** rhymes in the middle (often a middle word with the last word in a line)
50. **Near Rhyme:** almost rhymes
51. **Free Verse**: no rhyme
52. **Foot:** Pattern of stressed and unstressed <u>syllables</u>
53. **Meter:** (or *metre* in British spelling): "Repeat the <u>feet</u>" (or rhythm)
54. **Alliteration:** Repetition of a consonant sound at the beginning
55. **Consonance:** Repetition of a consonant sound in the middle ("Alliteration in the middle")
56. **Assonance:** Repetition of a vowel sound

D

Miscellaneous

57. **Infer:** To read or listen "between the lines" —to read something beyond the words
58. **Imagery:** Creates a <u>picture</u> with <u>words</u>
59. **Tone:** Writer (feeling writer tries to create in the text)
60. **Mood:** Reader (feeling reader experiences reading the text)
61. **Anecdote:** Short <u>(true) story</u> often funny or amusing
62. **Fable:** Story with <u>moral (or lesson)</u>, often starring animals
63. **Satire:** When someone is <u>angry</u> and <u>writes</u> something <u>humorous</u> to bring about <u>change</u>
64. **Legend:** Story from **PAST** that cannot be <u>proven</u>
65. **Myth:** Story that attempts to define the <u>world</u>, nature (usually cultural)
66. **Folktale:** Like a "baton," it's a cultural story "passed on" from generation to generation
67. **Situational Irony:** When you expect one thing to happen, but <u>the opposite happens</u>
    Example: A mechanic's car breaks down. (We expect his/her car to run properly.)
68. **Onomatopoeia:** Sound becomes a word
69. **Pseudonym:** AKA = also known as; an assumed name, like Dr. Seuss
70. **Allusion**: reference to a famous noun (person, place, thing, event...)
71. **Syntax:** Sentence fluency
72. **Diction:** Word choice
73. **Parallelism:** same structure (in lines or lists)
74. **Anaphora:** Parallelism "<u>same at the beginning</u>" (<u>different</u> <u>at the end</u>)
    Lincoln's Gettysburg Address: "But <u>we can not</u> <u>dedicate</u> – <u>we can not</u> <u>consecrate</u> – <u>we can not</u> <u>hallow</u> – this ground."
75. **Epistrophe:** Parallelism "same at the end" (different at the beginning)
    Lincoln's Gettysburg Address: "[...]<u> of</u> <u>the people,</u> by <u>the people,</u> <u>for</u> <u>the people</u>"

Figure 7.6 Poetry Analysis (Close Reading) Handout

Name: _____

Poetry Analysis
(Close Reading)

Directions: *Identify and label* the following literary devices in the poem below:

Alliteration	Oxymoron	Rhyme scheme	Imagery
Couplet	Personification	Simile	Metaphor
End Rhyme	Pun	Symbol	Refrain
Hyperbole	Internal rhyme	Quatrain	Onomatopoeia

The Flame

My mom is a candle of words
Whose heavy thoughts are light
But in the moment of dark I see her spark
And suddenly know what's right.

    Her example ignites the flame
    And I am no longer the same.

Like wax I drip from the frigid heat
A thousand suns smile with truth
And drop, drop, drop I seem to melt
In the fiery furnace of youth.

    Her faith fans the flame
    And I choose to go and do the same.

CB Taylor

144 ◆ Bonus Tool

Figure 7.7 Poetry Analysis (Close Reading) Answer Key

KEY   Name: _____

Poetry Analysis
(Close Reading)

Directions: *Identify and label* the following literary devices in the poem below:

Alliteration	Oxymoron	Rhyme scheme	Imagery
Couplet	Personification	Simile	Metaphor
End Rhyme	Pun	Symbol	Refrain
Hyperbole	Internal rhyme	Quatrain	Onomatopoeia

Note: Some terms occur more than once (and may not be marked).

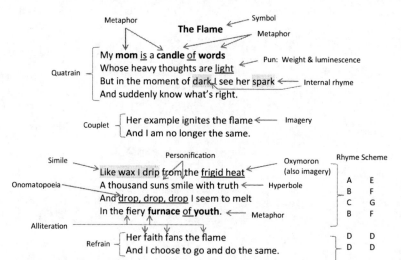

The Flame

Metaphor → (The Flame) ← Symbol
                              ↘ Metaphor

Quatrain:
My **mom** is a **candle** of words   ← Pun: Weight & luminescence
Whose heavy thoughts are light
But in the moment of dark I see her spark ← Internal rhyme
And suddenly know what's right.

Couplet:
Her example ignites the flame   ← Imagery
And I am no longer the same.

Simile → Like wax I drip from the frigid heat   ← Oxymoron (also imagery)
Onomatopoeia → A thousand suns smile with truth   ← Hyperbole
         And drop, drop, drop I seem to melt
         In the fiery furnace of youth.   ← Metaphor
Alliteration

Refrain:
Her faith fans the flame
And I choose to go and do the same.

Rhyme Scheme:
A   E
B   F
C   G
B   F
D   D
D   D

CB Taylor

Figure 7.8 Short Story Analysis (Close Reading) Handout

Name: _____

Short Story Analysis
(Close Reading)

Directions: <u>Identify and label</u> the following literary devices in the short story below:

Characters	Description of Characters	Rising Action
Setting	Description of Setting	Resolution (Lesson Learned)
Theme	Metaphor	Imagery
Dialogue	Conflict	Show, Don't Tell

Snakebite

My mom used to tell me, "Death is a part of life." I never really understood what that meant until one fateful day with my dog, Linus.

Summers in Arizona are sizzling, hot enough to see heat waves rising from the arid desert behind our house. Small bushes and grass patches fight for survival. Rocks line the wash that stretches out a stone's throw from my back yard. It's rarely ever filled, except during the monsoon season when rushes of water from the distant mountains gather to flow in dangerous torrents. My mom regularly warns me to be careful around the wash.

"Watch out for flash floods," she says. "And worse, watch out for snakes!" My mom is a petite woman. She stands 5'4" tall with brown shoulder-length hair and can be found wearing worn-out blue jeans most of the time. She has darker tanned skin, and callouses from working with a shovel in the yard. Even in the heat my dog Linus would join her. He was a noisy but loveable Chihuahua, often yapping at birds or evening joggers.

After a storm had subsided one summer afternoon, I heard a distinct YELP coming from the backyard. I could see Linus curiously barking at some dry desert branches, searching the pile as if he had found something. Suddenly, I my heart dropped! From my back window I could see the shape of

Figure 7.8 Continued

something frightening appear—a rattlesnake! I knew if Linus got too close, he could be bitten. I flung out the door, grabbing a shovel for protection. Overwhelmed by the adrenaline flowing through my veins, I didn't even think that I was placing myself in danger.

As I ran toward Linus, I could hear my mom shout, "What's going on? What is it?"

"A snake!" I mustered. I ran down the embankment but it was too late. Just as I was approaching, the retreating rattlesnake turned and swiped at Linus, biting him in the leg. Linus was clearly in shock and began to yelp in pain. My attention turned from the snake (that was now slithering away) to my friend, Linus, who had run away in terrible fright.

I was able to gather him up into my arms and rush him inside, where my mother joined me. I thought to myself: What should I do?

"What's the matter? Is he all right?" my mom blurted. I couldn't even respond. I don't know why, but I couldn't talk. It was as if my mouth was now the desert, waiting for a monsoon of feelings to rush down. And they did. I couldn't help it. I began to cry. The rains fell down my face when I could see that Linus was dying. The poison was too strong. Seconds later his breathing stopped.

I knew about death, but I didn't understand it before then. One moment, Linus was alive and happy. The next, he was in my arms motionless while I lie in my mom's arms. My mom was right: death is a part of life. It's a hard lesson to learn, but I'm grateful for Linus—and I'm grateful my mom was there when the lesson came.

By CB Taylor

Figure 7.9 Short Story Analysis (Close Reading) Answer Key

Name: _____

KEY

Short Story Analysis

Directions: <u>Identify and label</u> the following literary devices in the short story below:

Characters	Description of Characters	Rising Action
Setting	Description of Setting	Resolution (Lesson Learned)
Theme	Metaphor	Imagery
Dialogue	Conflict	Show, Don't Tell

Snakebite

(Theme arrow) (Characters arrow)
(Character arrow)
Setting ⤵

My mom used to tell me, "<u>Death is a part of life.</u>" I never really understood what that meant until one fateful day with my dog, Linus.

Summers in Arizona are sizzling, hot enough to see heat waves rising from the arid desert behind our house. Small bushes and grass patches fight for survival. Rocks line the wash that stretches out a stone's throw from my back yard. It's rarely ever filled, except during the monsoon season when rushes of water from the distant mountains gather to flow in dangerous torrents. My mom regularly warns me to be careful around the wash. — *Describes Setting*

Exposition

"Watch out for flash floods," she says. "And worse, watch out for snakes!" — *Dialogue*

My mom is a petite woman. She stands 5'4" tall with brown shoulder-length hair and can be found wearing worn-out blue jeans most of the time. She has darker tanned skin, and callouses from working with a shovel in the yard. — *Describes Mom*

Even in the heat my dog Linus would join her. He was a noisy but loveable Chihuahua, often yapping at birds or evening joggers. — *Describes Linus*

Conflict ⤵

<u>After a storm had subsided one summer afternoon, I heard a distinct YELP coming from the backyard. I could see Linus curiously barking at some dry desert branches, searching the pile as if he had found something. Suddenly, I my heart dropped! From my back window I could see the shape of</u>

Bonus Tool ◆ 147

Figure 7.9 Continued

Dialogue (Reminder: New speaker = New paragraph)

something frightening appear—a rattlesnake! I knew if Linus got too close, he could be bitten. I flung out the door, grabbing a shovel for protection. Overwhelmed by the adrenaline flowing through my veins, I didn't even think that I was placing myself in danger.

As I ran toward Linus, I could hear my mom shout, "What's going on? What is it?"

— Rising Action

"A snake!" I mustered. I ran down the embankment but it was too late. Just as I was approaching, the retreating rattlesnake turned and swiped at Linus, biting him in the leg. Linus was clearly in shock and began to yelp in pain. My attention turned from the snake (that was now slithering away) to my friend, Linus, who had run away in terrible fright.

I was able to gather him up into my arms and rush him inside, where my mother joined me. I thought to myself: What should I do? ← Climax

Shows sadness, doesn't tell sadness

"What's the matter? Is he all right?" my mom blurted. I couldn't even respond. I don't know why, but I couldn't talk. It was as if my mouth was now the desert, waiting for a **monsoon of feelings** to rush down. And they did. I couldn't help it. I began to cry. The **rains fell down my face** when I could see that Linus was dying. The poison was too strong. Seconds later his breathing stopped.

— Metaphor

Imagery

— Falling Action; Resolution

I knew about death, but I didn't understand it before then. One moment, Linus was alive and happy. The next, he was in my arms motionless while I lie in my mom's arms. My mom was right: death is a part of life. It's a hard lesson to learn, but I'm grateful for Linus—and I'm grateful my mom was there when the lesson came.

— Lesson Learned

By CB Taylor

Note: Some literary devices may be used more than once. Others not listed may also be present. This story is fictional. I only attached my name so that students could reference an author, an important skill if you have them write a response.

Appendix A
Thinking about Text: A Critical Thinking Map

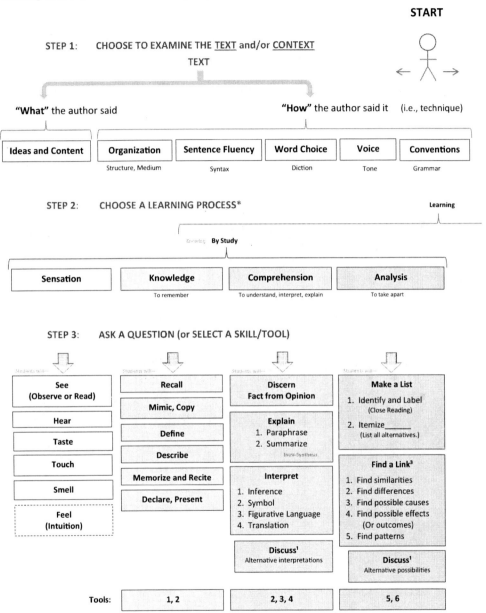

Appendix A Continued

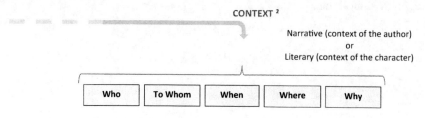
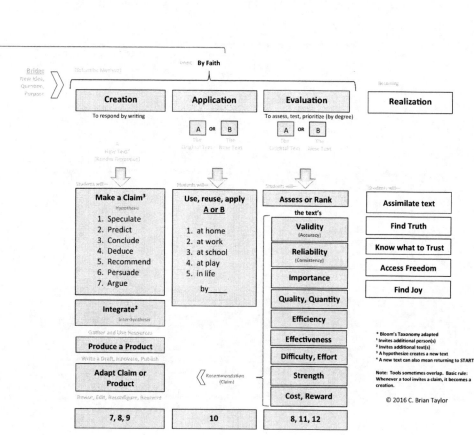

References

"Arizona Revised Statutes." Arizona Revised Statutes. N.p., n.d. Web. 4 Dec. 2015. http:www.azleg.state.az.us/ArizonaRevisedStatutes.asp?Title=13.

Armstrong, Patricia. "Bloom's Taxonomy." Center for Teaching, Vanderbilt University, 2015. Web. 24 Nov. 2015. https://cft.vanderbilt.edu/guides-sub-pages/blooms-taxonomy/.

Babbitt, Natalie. *Tuck Everlasting*. New York: Farrar, Straus, Giroux, 1975. Print.

Card, Orson Scott. *Ender's Game*. New York: Tor, 1991. Print.

Collodi, Carlo. "The Adventures of Pinocchio." The Project of Gutenberg EBook, 12 Jan. 2006. Web. 25 Nov. 2015. http://www.gutenberg.org/ebooks/500.

Curtis, Christopher Paul. *Bud, Not Buddy*. New York: Scholastic, 2000. Print.

———. *The Watsons Go to Birmingham—1963*. New York: Delacorte, 1995. Print.

Douglass, Frederick. "Holt McDougal Library, High School with Connections: Individual Reader." *Narrative of the Life of Frederick Douglass*. Austin, TX: Holt, Rinehart and Winston, n.d.

Frost, Robert. "The Road Not Taken. Frost, Robert. 1920. Mountain Interval." N.p., n.d. Web. 25 Nov. 2015. http://www.bartleby.com/119/1.html.

Henry, O. "The Ransom of Red Chief." The Literature Network, n.d. Web. 24 Nov. 2015. http://www.online-literature.com/donne/1041/.

Hinton, S.E. "The Outsiders." New York: Penguin Putnam, Inc., 1995, n.d. http://www.abrahamlincolnonline.org/lincoln/speeches/gettysburg.htm.

Jefferson, Thomas. "The Declaration of Independence." National Archives and Records Administration, n.d. Web. 24 Nov. 2015. http://www.archives.gov/exhibits/charters/declaration_transcript.html.

Kennedy, John. F. "1961–01–20 Inaugural Address." *Inaugural Address, 20, January 1961*. N.p., n.d. Web. 24 Nov. 2015. http://www.jfklibrary.org/Asset-Viewer/BqXIEM9F402ntF17SVAjA.aspx.

Key, Francis Scott. "The Lyrics." NMAH, N.p., n.d. Web. 25 Nov. 2015. http://amhistory.si.edu/starspangledbanner/the-lyrics.aspx.

King, Jr., Martin Luther. *Letter from Birmingham City Jail*. Philadelphia: American Friends Service Committee, May 1963. Print.

Lee, Harper. *To Kill a Mockingbird*. New York: Warner, 1982. Print.

Lincoln, Abraham. "The Gettysburg Address by Abraham Lincoln." *The Gettysburg Address by Abraham Lincoln*. N.p., n.d. Web. 24 Nov. 2015. http://www.abrahamlincolnonline.org/lincoln/speeches/gettysburg.htm.

Lowry, Lois. *The Giver*. New York: Bantam Doubleday Dell for Young Readers, 1993. Print.

Paulsen, Gary. *Hatchet*. New York: Bradbury, 1987. Print.

"Rest Area Sign Clip Art." Clkr.com, 22 Sept. 2011. Web. 8 Feb. 2016. http://www.clker.com/clipart-147261.html.

Rowling, J.K. *Harry Potter and the Sorcerer's Stone*. New York: Scholastic Press, 1998. Print.

Sachar, Louis. *Holes*. New York: Farrar, Straus and Giroux, 1998. Print.

Shakespeare, William. "Romeo and Juliet." *Elements of Literature, Third Course*. Beers, G. Kylene and Lee Odell (Eds.). Austin, TX: Holt, Rinehart and Winston, 2005. Print.

Spinelli, Jerry. *Stargirl*. Toronto: Scholastic, 2000. Print.

Straub, Richard. "Teacher Response as Conversation: More than Casual Talk, an Exploration." *Rhetoric Review*. 14, No. 2 (Spring, 1996), 374–399.

Taylor, C. Brian. "Driving the Text." 2016. Print.

———. "The Flame." 2015. Print.

———. "Snakebite." 2015. Print.

Twain, Mark. *The Adventures of Tom Sawyer*. Mineola, NY: Dover Publications, 1998. Print.

Wiggins, Grant, and McTighe, Jay. *Understanding by Design*. Expanded 2nd ed. Pearson, 2006. Print.

Index

The Adventures of Tom Sawyer 106, 125–6
agree or disagree 14, 34, 44, 106
alliteration 139
All Tools at Once 12, 32, 42
allusion 140
analysis (*see* analyze)
Analysis: Cause and Effect (*see* Cause and Effect)
Analysis: Close Reading (*see* Close Reading)
Analysis: Compare-Contrast (*see* Compare-Contrast)
Analysis: Correlation (*see* Correlation)
Analysis: Find a Link (*see* Find a Link)
Analysis: Itemizing (*see* Itemizing)
Analysis: Key Words 62
Analysis: Make a List (*see* Make a List)
analyze 61, 69
anaphora 140
anecdote 140
Another's Point of View 27
Application 27–8, 106
archetype 138
Ask a Question 3, 5
assonance 139

Babbit, Natalie 106, 122
Better or Worse 29–30
Bloom, Benjamin (*see* Bloom's Taxonomy)
Bloom's Taxonomy 2–5, 7, 23–30, 49
Bud, Not Buddy 106, 118–19

Card, Orson Scot 106, 114–15
Cause and Effect 20–1, 23, 38–9, 106
change 13
character 106
characterization 138
Choose a Learning Process 2–3
Cinderella 73–81
cinquain 139
claim (*see* topic sentences)
cliché 137
climax 138
Close Reading 17
Collodi, Carlo 59–61
Compare-Contrast 19, 23, 38, 106
Comprehension: *Gettysburg Address* 103
conditional (*see* If . . ., then . . .)
conflict 138
conflict types 138
connotation 137
consonance 139
context 1–2, 59, 68
conventions 106
correlation 21–3, 38, 106
couplet 139
Creating a Claim 4, 12
Critical Thinking Map (Children's Version) 6–7
Critical Thinking Map (Teacher's Version) 3, 149–50
Crossing the Bridge 4
Cue Cards 135
Curtis, Christopher Paul 106, 116–19

Declaration of Independence 106, 127–8
denotation 137

dialogic context (*see* context)
dialogue 138
diction 140
Doing (by Faith) 2–3
Douglass, Frederick 106–10
Driving the Text 6–7

Education Northwest 1
Effective-Ineffective 28, 35, 45
empathy (*see* Another's Point of View)
Ender's Game 106, 114–15
end rhyme 139
epistrophe 140
epithet 137
euphemism 137
evaluation 106
Evaluation: Better or Worse (*see* Better or Worse)
Evaluation: Identifying Qualities (*see* Rubric, Identifying Qualities)
Evaluation: Optional Scales (*see* Optional Scales)
Evaluation: Prioritizing or Assessing (*see* Ranking)
Evaluation: Validity & Reliability of a Text (*see* Validity and Reliability)
evidence (*see* quote)
Evidence Finder (Introduced) 57–8
Evidence Finder Options 62–4
example (*see* claim)
Explain the Quote 68, 77, 103
exposition 138

fable 140
falling action 138
figurative language 137
Find a Link 18, 38–9
The Flame 143–4
folktale 140
foot 139

foreshadowing 138
free verse 139
Frost, Robert 46, 53–4

Gettysburg Address 73, 96–104, 142; *see also* Comprehension, Gettysburg Address
The Giver 73, 91–6
Goldilocks and the Three Bears 73, 82–5

Harry Potter and the Sorcerer's Stone 44–5
Hatchet 73, 86–91
Henry, O. 106, 132–3
Hinton, S.E. 106, 111–12
Holes 106, 120
hyperbole 137
hypothetical (*see* If . . ., then . . .)

Identifying Qualities (*see* Rubric, Identifying Qualities)
idiom 137
If . . ., then . . . 23–5
imagery 140
Inaugural Address (JFK 1961) 106, 134
infer 57, 140
inference (*see* infer)
irony 106
irony, situational 140
irony, verbal 137
itemizing 17

Jefferson, Thomas 106, 127–8

Kennedy Jr., John, F. 106, 134
Key, Francis Scott 106, 130–1
King Jr., Martin Luther 106, 129
knowing (by study) 2–3

learning 3
Learning Process (*see* Choose a Learning Process)

Lee, Harper 106, 113
legend 140
Letter from Birmingham Jail 106, 129
Lincoln, Abraham 61, 73, 96–104, 142
literary context 59
literary devices 106
literary terms (*see* Cue Cards; literary devices)
literary terms packet (*see* Cue Cards)
Lowery, Louis 73, 91–6

Make a List 17
man *vs.* (*see* conflict types)
metaphor 137
meter 139
mood 140
motif 138
multi-quote 71–2
multi-source (*see* multi-quote)
myth 140

narrative context (*see* context)
Narrative of the Life of Frederick Douglass: An American Slave 106–10
near rhyme 139
Northwest Regional Educational Laboratory (*see* Education Northwest)
NWREL (*see* Education Northwest)

One-page Tool Sheets 11–13
One Tool at a Time 11
onomatopoeia 140
Optional Scales 29
organization 106
The Outsiders 106, 111–12

parallelism 140
Paraphrase (*see* Explain the Quote)
Paulsen, Gary 73, 86–91
personification 137

perspective (*see* Another's Point of View)
Pinocchio 59–61
plot diagram 138
poetry 139; *see also The Flame*
point of view 138
prose 139
pseudonym 140
pun 137

quatrain 139
Question Starters 8–10
quote 59, 68

Ranking 30–2
The Ransom of Red Chief 106, 132–3
realization 3–5
refrain 139
resolution 138
rhyme scheme 139
rising action 138
The Road Not Taken 46, 53–4
Romeo and Juliet 69–71
Rowling, J.K. 44–5
Rubric: Identifying Qualities 32

Sachar, Louis 106, 120
satire 140
Says This, Means That 15–16
The Secret Recipe 66
See, Don't See 13, 34, 44
Selecting a Skill 5
sensation 3–5
Shakespeare, William 69–71
short answer 67
Should-Would-Could 26
show, don't tell 138
simile 137
situational irony 140
Snakebite 145–8
Spinelli, Jerry 106, 123–4

stacking 5
stanza 139
Stargirl 106, 123–4
Star Spangled Banner 106, 130–1
supporting paragraph 67
Sweeney, Alysee 73, 82–5
symbol 106, 137
synecdoche 137
syntax 140

Taylor, C. Brian 143–4
tercet 139
text 1
text-to-self 63, 106
theme 106, 138
Thinking About Text: A Critical Thinking Map (*see* Critical Thinking Map (Children's Version); Critical Thinking Map (Teacher's Version))
Thinking Frame (Blank Template) 50
Thinking Frame (Photo Analysis–Blank Template) 51
Thinking Frame (Photo Analysis–KEY) 52
Thinking Frame (Problem Analysis–Blank Template) 55
Thinking Frame (Problem Analysis–KEY) 56
Thinking Frame (Text Analysis–Blank Template) 53
Thinking Frame (Text Analysis–KEY) 54
To Kill a Mockingbird 106, 113
tone 97, 140
Tool Templates 36, 42–3
topic (*see* topic sentences)
topic sentences 12, 59, 68, 75–6
Tuck Everlasting 106, 122
Twain, Mark 106, 125–6
The 12 Tools: All Tools at Once (*see* All Tools at Once)
The 12 Tools: One-page Tool Sheets (*see* One-page Tool Sheets)
The 12 Tools: One Tool at a Time (*see* One Tool at a Time)

understatement 137

validity and reliability 33
verse 139
viraling 136

The Watsons Go to Birmingham, 1963 106, 116–17